Contents

Preface

Embodying Otherness is the first of three editions on Theatrum Mundi's long term interest in choreography, embodiment and urban design. Since its inception in 2012, Theatrum Mundi has worked with choreographers, dancers and engineers, exploring and analysing choreographic and architectural thinking. We have organised events, run experimental workshops and acted as a platform to disseminate our own research and share the ideas and projects of collaborators and fellows from the same or different disciplines.

This first edition thus marks a moment of introspection: revisiting Theatrum Mundi's archive, sorting through its content, picking out pieces, de- and re- contextualising them by bringing them into dialogue, and placing them alongside newly-commissioned thought pieces and contemporary practices. It is our intention to speculatively lay the groundwork for what can be a discussion of the built environment through embodied experiences and we very much hope that you see, just as we do, each of these short pieces as small but powerful provocations to make you question, think, debate and reflect. Owing intellectual debt to Siobhan Davis for the idea of meshwork, we approached the archive as an assembly of works in different formats, belonging to different authors from within and outside the organisation. The nine selected archival works vary in length and composition, but share one thing in common: they, in one way or another, think of, with and through bodies when talking about cities. Together with four newly commissioned pieces, they propose an embodied understanding of power, politics, rules, mobility, interactions, rhythm, temporality, presence and identity. These works are loosely connected thematically, chronologically

and stylistically, yet arranged into four themes: *Force*, *Codes*, *Flux* and *Contingencies*. These should not be seen as thinking silos but rather as framings which bleed into each other, both intellectually and visually, throughout the whole book. These themes were formulated by Rebecca Faulkner during her 2020 research placement with Theatrum Mundi as a means to imagine new alternate realities through performative and choreographed lenses. The last section of the publication foregrounds six propositional projects as alternative approaches and possibilities for bridging the performative potentials of choreography into architecture. This is only the beginning of what, we think, can be a useful directory of interdisciplinary spatial practices. In the following two editions, we will continue expanding our research on choreographic thinking in city-making as a member of the European Future Architecture Platform.

We are very grateful to all the contributors for their creativity, dedication and collaboration in this journey despite the difficulties of the current time. We also would like to thank our contributing designers, Marcos Villalba and Cecily Chua, who visually strengthened the conceptual content, and Rebecca Faulkner who was the catalyst and driving force behind this first edition. Without them, our editorial thinking and process would not have managed to highlight the quality and depth in the various pieces.

We hope that you allow yourselves to indulge in the little variations of this composition with your minds, hearts and bodies.

Elahe Karimnia and Fani Kostourou
June 2021

Introduction

Embodying Otherness asks what kind of questions or discussions in city-making may necessitate an engagement of choreographic thinking? How can an understanding of our bodily senses, functions, movements and intellect contribute to an augmented ability to speculate on future city-dwelling?

The body has long been at the centre of political struggle; our movements on an individual and collective scale have deep, complex and contested histories. Our ability – or inability – to move through certain places and spaces transforms us from bystanders into active citizens.[1] The presence of our bodies and the length of time we can be still, belong, occupy or feel connected to the built environment are our basic civil rights. In this sense, our bodies become fleshy sites in which the micro- and macropolitics and socio-cultural codes are mediated, revealing injustices in our movement and our unequally distributed rights to stay or dwell in a place.[2] The body is a conflicted territory, a living archive of the historical, political, social, cultural and environmental struggles we have endured.

In Bodily Cartographies, Blanca Pujals – a contributor to this edition – articulates how since the Enlightenment, 'the body' has merged with urban planning to create and reinforce *the normalised body*. Ironically, this body, for whom the city has been built, is rarely an inclusive one. Historically, societal and spatial conditions have established white, sanitary and predominantly male able bodies as the appropriate ones to occupy public space.[3] By default, those who fall outside of such 'standards', have been unjustly labelled as *others,* and considered to pose a threat to society. This contested view has over the years escalated phenomena of social withdrawal, exclusion and expulsion, whether through formal laws or informal acts that seek to prohibit basic rights of participation, convening or protest.

'Where we are makes a difference to what we can know'.[4] Yet, what has been afforded to us by society is based on the bodies we happen to inhabit, following constructed norms that we, one way or another, adhere to. Our human body is a social construct, 'a site not just of cultural endeavour but also a site of self-appropriation and adaptation'.[5] The body manifests, challenges and re-explores the interrelation between location, identity and knowledge to suggest an epistemological condition and a kind of knowingness that refuses fixity.[6] Navigating the unknown and otherness, resisting and appropriating itself to the ebb and flow of the city and all its cohabiting species: this is the crux of embodiment. As perspectives on embodiment reveal, it is not *about* the body per se, it is about the culture and the experiences we build within our environments and express in our acts, from the standpoint of *being in the world*.[7]

As cities are predominantly created by the built environment professionals, they are naturally designed for, or from, the perspective of those professionals' lived experience. But, if their training fails to equip them with the skills to understand or critique the social or environmental implications of said designs,[8] there is a risk that our cities will never be reflective of the complexity of all of our lived experiences. This is amplified when the authority given to the designers and other decision-makers is not challenged or accountable. The shocking lack of diversity within the built environment professions has traditionally served to perpetuate this narrative. As of March 2021, Architects Registration Board (ARB) showed that the number of white, able-bodied and male architects has been disproportionately high among practitioners in the UK.[9] And, in May 2020, Southwark Council appointed 110 practices for their new architectural framework, yet none were led by black architects, despite 46% of the borough identifying as non-white and 25% of it as black.[10]

So, how can the role of city-making be reflective of our wider society? How can existing architectural and urban practices be redefined to embrace *otherness* and all embodied experiences? Both acts of expansion and redefinition being, quite literally, about opening up to other professions, disciplines and ways of knowing, designing and building.

However, acknowledging *otherness,* be that in bodies or professions, without acknowledging *othering* is not the intention here. The *otherness* we refer to is not a process of alienation or an 'us' versus 'them' mentality, expressed in the sociological term of 'othering'. Rather, it is the ways and means of doing things differently, embracing non-confirmative ways of seeing and making the city, and thinking with the language of our bodies to contemplate the city 'with all our bodily senses, not just the eyes and intellect.'[11]

Embodying Otherness, therefore, is a counter-hegemonic method of viewing and acting in cities, that combines many forms of media beyond academia, while seeking to elevate subaltern, feminist, black, indigenous and queer voices. The collection is so far inspired and shaped by creative practices, choreographic-thinking, theoretical and critical inquiries offered by artists, architects, choreographers, engineers, designers and academics commissioned by or for Theatrum Mundi within the last few years.

In this strange and isolating time, we hope this publication helps us reconnect with both the idea and the reality of 'the body'. Let us undo, let us redo, let us contemplate 'what if', let us be attentive for each other and the city.

1   Onomatopee (2020) "RIGHTS OF WAY: The body as witness in public space" [www.onomatopee.net/ exhibition/ rights-of-way/]
2   Sheller, M. (2018) *Mobility Justice: The Politics of Movement in an Age of Extremes.*
3   Pujals, B. (2016) Bodily Cartographies: Pathologizing the Body and the City, *The Funambulist: Health Struggles* [https://thefunambulist.net/magazine/ health-struggles]
4   Rendell, J. (2007) *Site-Writing, Enigma and Embellishment.*
5   Borden, K, Rendell, Pilvar et al. (2000), *The Unknown City: Contesting Architecture and Social Space.*
6   Following postmodern feminism and new ways of knowing and being; see for example the work by Haraway, D. (1998) 'Situated knowledges: the science question in feminism and the privilege of partial knowledge' or Braidotti, R. (1994) 'Nomadic Subjects'.
7   Csordas, T.J. (1999) "Embodiment and Cultural Phenomenology" in Weiss, G. and Haber, H. F. (eds.) *Perspectives on Embodiment.*
8   Cosgrave, E. (2019), "The feminist City", Ted Talk. [www.ted.com/talks/dr_ellie_cos- grave_the_ feminist_city
9   Architects Registration Board (2021), *Equality & Diversity Data,* [https://arb.org.uk/about-arb/ equality-diversity/data/]
10 Green, B. (2019) "Grounds for optimism in improving profession's diversity", *The RIBA Journal.* [www.ribaj. com/intelligence/market-analysis-statistics-gender-ethnicity-socio-economic-background-architects]
11 Borden, K, et al. (2000) *The Unknown City: Contesting Architecture and Social Space.*

Rebecca Faulkner
and Elahe Karimnia

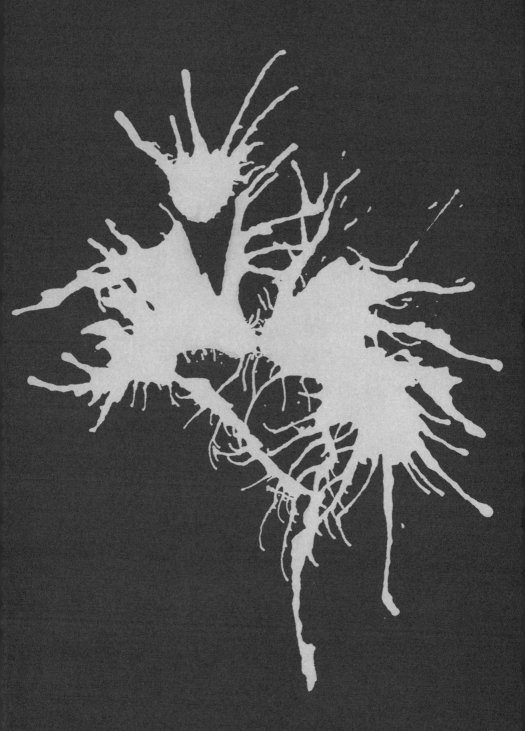

FORCE focuses on the power and surveillance of the body, bringing to the fore discussions around mobility, justice and scale. Through this theme, not only do we question who the city is for, but we also wish to challenge who is considered valuable in society; who has power and autonomy over their bodies; who is the observer and who is the subject of observation; who has the right to move at a global scale and how power is forcibly enacted on bodies across the globe.
In light of the ever-growing restrictions on our civil liberties – extended policing powers and laws that quash our rights to protest or convene – it is increasingly pertinent to examine how we can protect the right to occupy space.

Performing Violence

Based on a transcript of a conversation recorded for Theatrum Mundi Live in April 2020 between Paul Setúbal and Elahe Karimnia. The podcast was produced by Andrea Cetrulo.

Speakers: Elahe Karimnia, Paul Setúbal, Andrea Cetrulo.

E

Urban design practices, generally, misconceive and underestimate embodied experiences; and the way bodies in cities have to adapt to the norms and rules within the built environment has become naturalised. I would like to reverse this relation and ask what if norms were following bodies? How can manifested powers on bodies help adjust the design principles? In your work, Paul, you perform these embodied powerful experiences, particularly in public space. Could you tell us more about that?

P   I am very interested in this archetype of masculinity and these ideas of violation and dominance related to my upbringing on the outskirts of Brasília. We are born with images of violence surrounding us. Through performance and art, I show how police gestures and military moves are incarnated in our body, without acting violently. I use these powerful gestures against the power, as a way to challenge and discuss power, control and domination.

E

This power of control and domination that you mentioned also exists in the built environment. The architecture is also a gesture that can demonstrate power, imposed on bodies. What do you think of the different levels of power? Sometimes, power is readable, tangible and materialised and sometimes it just creates an ambience and can be perceived by some people. How do you consider these levels and types of power?

A   How do you conceptualise these differences in the different contexts you lived, Paul?

P   In São Paulo you always need to cover your back to protect yourself and the violence on the street changes your body; for example, you cross the street to avoid confrontation with police. Body is an intelligent machine and always plans ways to escape violence. This experience was different in London in the beginning. Later I realised London is a city with many surveillance cameras like CCTVs. My body started to feel this sensation and act differently. In Brasilia the architecture creates an atmosphere of power. The city was designed as a utopian city, not a city for people. There are no statues or monuments because the entire city is a monument in itself. You feel the sensation of this political power across your body. So, the power is presented differently in each city and the body reacts to it accordingly.

E

It is interesting how abstract power is materialised in different forms, from monumental buildings and CCTVs to the presence of police. Each form creates different kinds of exclusion, spatially and socially, by setting restrictions on our daily behaviours and actions. The level of power which is not tangible but perceived by some bodies, depending on their experiences, has been challenged less. In Sweden where I lived for almost a decade, the level of freedom in moving around the city is impressive. You are allowed to enter and walk in any non-private land, including all public spaces and public buildings. I grew up in Tehran, where the presence of police in public space, and at the entrance of any public building, has been naturalised. As you mentioned, Paul, I also felt a sense of freedom in my body when I moved to Stockholm, before I got to know the socio-cultural norms. Through my own research, I found that such provided freedoms, and also publicness of space, do not necessarily result in individuals taking over the space or appropriating it. The absence of materialised power does not necessarily mean empowering bodies or at least all different bodies.

P   The system creates tangible or, as you mentioned Elahe, intangible mechanisms of control over bodies. For example, monuments, which are usually landmarks in cities, are locked with bars in São Paulo to expel the presence of the body next to them. People still wait next to a monument as a meeting point but far from it. I am really interested in how the body can challenge these barriers that architecture or the system create. It's beautiful how the body takes possession of architecture.

A   And perhaps how the body hacks space?

E

There are many examples of how the rules and spatial norms are contested in everyday use of space. Sometimes, just being present and still in urban space is powerful and challenging enough. Presence can challenge prohibiting signs or even expected behaviours. Yet, the right of presence is not always and fully experienced. It takes a lot of effort or even courage to just be in public space and resist what is expected. How do you show such resistance in your performance, Paul?

P   Two years ago in 2018, I was invited for a performance during an Art Fair (SP Arte), which took place inside the pavilion of the Bienal de São Paulo. The building was the most important part of the art fair; a heritage building redesigned by Oscar Niemeyer, like a living monument. In my performance Compensation for Excess I tried to expose two power structures of the Art Fair: first, the building and second, the system and its untouched hidden power. The system always puts a lot of pressure on the body and the body always has to resist. It is the body–of the artist–that has to deal with the system; the body is the most fragile part of a system. I used my body weight to hold a very important and expensive Brazilian piece of art suspended in the air for five days, as a metaphor to show that my body holds and controls the system, which is much more powerful. If the art piece fell, I would be literally destroyed. I had a small budget to produce the performance and I had to pay part of the production and insurance from my pocket. And that was also the idea of the performance; to show such hidden power structure, that people are mostly concerned about the building and the piece of art to be safe, concerned about the audience to be safe, but not the body of the artist – that is always the last concern and the most fragile part of the system. The power of the art, to me, is to push things to the edge, to face problems and to expose hidden information.

E

It makes me think of places in the city that are economically precious sites, such as business districts or shopping malls, where the least of concerns is about people who maintain them, keeping them clean and running. In fact, some people are *unexpected* in these areas. For example, I've written about the Filipino migrants – historically domestic workers for Hong Kong families – whose weekly gathering in the city centre challenged the historical power structure as well as the newly designed semi-public space of HSBC Bank. Their presence in the city centre was not a problem, but 'taking over the space' for their activities, gathering, networking and supporting each other by giving services such as doing nails in that part of the city, were not expected. These minority citizens had access to spaces which, as you mentioned, Paul, should be kept safe. Their presence and appropriation of public spaces unmask the socio-political exclusions of these bodies. We just talked about what design can do and we should rather ask: how design can empower the act of presence in public spaces? Can you give us an example by which performance could challenge the notion of citizenship, presence and public space management?

P   In 2014, with my collective Grupo EmpreZa, we did an exhibition in Rio de Janeiro at Museu de Arte do Rio. The spaces around the museum were under transformation towards the Olympics and lots of destruction and construction was going on; and people were really unhappy about it because they were being displaced, for example. This situation inspired us for a two-day performance. On the first day, we acted like construction workers and spent a whole day constructing a square of cement; and on the second day, we acted like a living statue holding tools, spending almost two hours silently just being on that square and at the end we started to destroy the square. It was like a public demonstration of the destruction of this new building because the performance happened just in front of the museum. Through performing long hours, the people started to watch and to became part of the performance. They took the tools and started to destroy the square and then they continued: "we need to destroy the museum... it causes a lot of trouble for us ...". We challenged the management mechanism because performance was permitted, destruction not, and that's the reality.

A   How do you think of violence and its materialised forms? As something that can be porous, visible, invisible, soft gestures, or hidden?

E

The use of materials is a powerful way by which designers can affect users' perceptions and experiences. There are examples that hostile design is employed as a solution for 'safe' public spaces, for example, which in reality means to intentionally restrict certain types or duration of activities, such as using metal for designing urban furniture in cold or even hot climates. Empowering design, as I said before, is a care to the public.

P   I am very interested in the design of tools and objects of power. There is a fine line between violence and pleasure. All these tools of power or toys of pleasure are used to dominate and control. The design of these objects is very similar. Police holding a baton is like a guy holding a big dildo because both objects are to demonstrate power. I am very interested in the line between control, domination and pleasure because I think most of the people who work with power have a lot of pleasure from it; it is like an addiction.

E

Your approach to violence, by performing its gestures, movements and pace, as well as tools and materials, unmasks a network of power over people and their bodies, which provides authority and enables acts of violence to create an atmosphere of fear. Designers, in a different way, have such authority to frame places and to manage micro-power dynamics. Performing power is a great embodied method for urban practices to understand how designed spaces, buildings and material objects, as well as management signs and rules are performed in people's everyday life. Performance, as you discussed, its temporariness but effectiveness, can interrupt urban design's very conventional thinking and approaches: 'what else' could be done, and 'how else' could we do it.

P   When you watch a performance, you can translate that experience to the body. I create a distanced experience for people to watch me hitting the wall and hearing gunshots, etc. to show that the act of violence is hurtful, loud and absurd; they do nothing. Also, through performance, I try to cross the line of what is understood as taboo. For example, we proposed a performance with fire in a museum. Of course, it is impossible to have a fire in the museum. But we made possible a proposal to cross this taboo and people really enjoyed it.

E

Yes, in most of your performances, you showed us how to cross the line of possibilities, for example through your choice of site or stage to challenge the ongoing hidden power dynamics. This is an inspiring point for us, as designers of the urban environment, to think about our authority, practiced through our choices of sites or materials, to maintain the power dynamics or to use the creativity of design to constructively challenge them.

Social Movement: Stage and Street

How do people move their bodies in political protests, on city streets and on stage? This question set out for a discussion of choreography in society followed by conversations derived from watching four video clips on social movement.

The first clip was The Social Life of Small Urban Spaces by American urbanist and sociologist William H. Whyte in 1980. What was striking was a graph that shows that interactions within squares almost always take place near the perimeter – and never at the centre – of the square.

'Blankness is too open, vulnerable and uneasy, whereas the textured space provides something to relate to, or against, to which to respond, engage, prompting a more evolutionary, organic use of public space. Prescription in public space is often problematic or just doesn't work, but suggestion of use can be wonderful.' (Excerpt from a reflection by Laura Raicovich, workshop participant).

After the second clip: Tahrir: Liberation Square, a documentary by director and cinematographer Stefano Savona released in 2011, the discussion was mostly of two strands. The first was about the rhythms present in the Egyptian chants and how a culture of poetry perhaps lends itself towards this form of communication and display within the square. There was much talk about the relatively simple chants that came out of the 'Occupy Movement' in the U.S., and how, belonging to a much more visual culture, Americans have a similar level of display in the signs they use. The second strand of thought was about the location of these occupations, such as Tahrir Square and Zuccotti Park, that are spaces not designed for displays as such. The fact that these spaces were not designed for such events makes them even more appealing for these types of gatherings.

Another clip was City of Abstracts by Bill Forsythe, which led to contrasting opinions about the intervention in Germany and the meaning of participation. From one perspective, the fluid mirrors of the piece showed individuals infatuated with their own reflections in public. Another perspective saw the displays of the fluid movement of the participants as being motivated by the video effect and felt that their participation was a performance of sorts for the others in public. This led to a deeper conversation about silliness and/or the over-sincerity of social movements – both of which can undermine a cause – and their difficult relationship with design. The struggle between a spontaneous and a choreographed, pre-meditated performance was strong throughout the conversation.

The last clip was part of a dance, choreographed by Theatrum Mundi's fellow, Siobhan Davies, which focused on walking. This video brought back the most basic form of public movement, as seen in the first clip by William H. Whyte, but married it with the choreographed form of dance. The conversation on designing for occupation or other social interventions continued with questions about designing a public space. The same questions were framed as prescription versus design that is made to be incomplete until the actors complete it – though very likely in a way that cannot be known in advance. The idea that a space must be designed ready for its own destruction became stronger.

A reflection by Theatrum Mundi, organiser of the 'Social Movement' workshop in New York in April 2012.

How does the city move you?
On bodies, identity and urban design

Our cities are built based on generalised ideas about human bodies and how they move. What if choreography could challenge these assumptions and help urban design thinking and practice imagine more diverse identities?

How does the city move you event brought researchers and practitioners from the disciplines of urbanism and dance into dialogue to explore how choreographic thinking could inform urban design and planning, broadening our understanding of the relationships between bodies, movement and the city.

The event started with two discussions: how architecture imagines the body, and how different cultures of movement can resist this. The first part of the discussion: 'Imagined Bodies', focused on exploring what kind of urban body is assumed? what physical identities is the city designed around? and how can choreographic thinking help imagine and articulate other kinds of physicality? The second part of the discussion was about understanding cultures of movement and how shapes and rhythms are formed in the social life of cities. How do queer or migrant cultures of movement, for example, inhabit the city?

These discussions were followed by three parallel workshops: (a) Choreographing the City: at the City Limits explored where choreographic and architectural problems meet, collide and inform each other; (b) Walking Latin Elephant approached the relationship between bodies, representation, memory and identity – walking through the London neighbourhood of Elephant & Castle, the aim was to experience what it means to inhabit a space and how our senses embrace cities; and (c) Vogue-Chi, a multigenerational queer and allies' safe space for self-expression and coming together.

The day ended with performance-based interventions by dance artists from Candoco Dance Company who challenge and broaden perceptions of art and ability, and place people and collaboration at the heart of their work. They were in residence at the Siobhan Davies Studio for five days during June 2018. The artists researched their own embodied relationship to identity and urban design in and around the Studio, and some of them, during the events, performed pieces that were closely entangled with and informed by the studio building itself.

An event organised in June 2018 by Theatrum Mundi partnered with Siobhan Davies Dance, UCL City Leadership Laboratory, and Candoco Dance Company at Siobhan Davies Studios in London as part of the London Festival of Architecture.

Taking Them Down

She was swatting neo-Nazi
with her handbag...

...But they were concerned,
it [her sculpture] could be interpreted
as promoting violence...

The unveiling of the sculpture *The woman with the Handbag – Kvinnan med Handväskan* – in Sweden was rather controversial. The statue, based on a photograph taken in 1985 in Sweden,[1] depicts a woman hitting a marching neo-Nazi with her handbag. The march was planned and approved by the Swedish authority, after the Left Party's leader gave a speech. Although the photograph received international attention and awards, the presence of a life-size statue of the woman, thirty years later, as a public memorial of the confrontation created nationwide controversy, and was opposed.[2] To protest the decision, people across Sweden began hanging handbags on statues;[3] embodying memories and debates that never got the chance to be present in the city.

Whose body has the power and political agency of being present in the city, confronting or provoking the forces limiting their presence, temporarily or timelessly? Once a body stands alone in public, it is not alone; there are stories, controversial and partial, hidden in that very presence, in its

intentions, imaginations and materiality. It is a silence before a speech or action.[4] Standing still in public space has interruptive potentials. Its stillness, in any form, interrupts the moment, the comfort of anonymity. Its stillness is an invitation; an invitation to a pause, a moment of attentiveness; an invitation to actions, movements, and to confront the powers embedded silently in that place, in that moment, in that pause, with different temporality, five minutes or five decades.

As I hold the front pages of two newspapers in my hand, one published in December 2017 in Iran and the other in June 2020 in the UK, I look at two bodies. Their stillness in the street capture one as a living body of a woman in a special pose raising a white cloth, and the other as an effigy of a man on a plinth standing pensively. Both were later taken down. The headlines raised concerns about her intentions in that pose and about those who were about to topple him down. What follows is a poem that offers a space tracing their presence backwards and tracking their absence forwards, thereby bringing to the fore the debates and forces swirling around the continuum of the two bodies,[5] two cities, and two political sites in time.

A poem by Elahe Karimnia, as a new contribution in response to the theme of *Force*.

She stands,
where the statues
of public figures are stolen
from public space
by ruling powers

                    He stands
              where racism is a
              common history
                  on pedestal

a decisive moment of
confrontation
              a silent landmark of heroism

        Taking them down!

                              Moved slowly, decisively,
                              ignored the veiled minds, heads,
                              hidden realities, everything that ignored
                              her being.

                                        A decent man,
                              with cane and knee-breeches
                              in his flowing wig, velvet coat,
                                        was staged.

                              She crawled up swiftly,
                              that 1.4m electric box – cold and dusty
                              she was up, standing quietly.

                                   On a 3.2m plinth of Portland
                              stone, with marine horses, mermaids
                              and anchors, he stands wise and virtuous.

                              Unknown, nameless.

                                        Eternally vigorous.

Stood still, in silence,
no smile, no voice, a lost status,
her eyes, her gaze, her hope – stolen.

Withdrawn and pensive,
looking down to his illustrious past.
A crying shame
is drowned in the harbour,
in his frown lines, lines of pain, no wonder!

Waved her white cotton headscarf
on a stick in the air,
liberating
her mind,
her being,
her hair.
In her own adlocutio pose,
raised her arm,
yet no command, no patrons.

Enriched in bronze a white history,
an inherited victory,
a bittersweet glory.

Declares through her
nothing but
a female body,
a mother,
a daughter,
a ruled,
disregarded, marginalised body.

She is shaking
the minds of those reading
her being: "improper, unauthorised".

Engraved in his plinth,
the harbour,
the love of trade, no wonder.
Silenced, enslaved, transported bodies,
across the ocean,
no ponder.

A living body
in a devoted pose,
no glance to right or left,
        no glance to those
pointing at her,
taking photos.
She's breathing
the unexplored seconds,
living the unknown: how it ends.

In a city built on
his wealth and fame,
he is a dead figure
acclaimed with no shame,
of sanitised history,
untold colonial past,
of enslaved bodies across the ocean
left to be at last.

Her presence grants a troubled site,
crafting resistance.

His presence confirms a
buried racism, crafting dissension.

In that space of refusal,
In that prolonged uncomfortable history,
In that moment of interruption,

they become foreground.
And the time comes when performance ends
and history begins.

Taking them
down!

Policemen –
vociferous, with raised arms,
her living body in their hands.

People –
clamorous with raised arms
his empty bronze body in their rope.

forceful, abrupt
pulled ruthlessly,
dragged assertively.

Came down she
with shouts and tears.

Came down he
too easy with rain of cheers.

"where is she taken?" – cries and fears.
next on the plinth, who will appear?

a thug?

an act thuggery?

"why"– is not a valid question here.
who decides "what is valid here?"

Her silent voice,
her forceful pose,
her courage,
reverberated.
Girl of Enghelab Street
standing still,
here, there
one after another,
"courage calls to courage everywhere"[6]

Black Lives Matter
a dark utter
writes a common history
with bodies that
equally matter.

This poem has a place,
in troubled histories, in troubled bodies,
staged and erected,
defaced, removed, pulled,
and relocated.

What goes up must go down
for delayed democracy
for uncomfortable history.

1   The photograph was taken in Växjö, Sweden on 13 April 1985 by photojournalist Hans Runesson, during a small demonstration of The Nordic Realm Party supporters.

2   Noack, R. (2015) "Sweden blocks plan to honor woman who hit a neo-Nazi with a purse". *The Washington Post* [www.washingtonpost.com/news/worldviews/wp/2015/02/28/sweden-blocks-plan-to-honor-woman-who-hit-a-neo-nazi-with-a-purse/]

3   Staff (2015) "Statue handbag protest takes off". Sverige Radio [https://sverigesradio.se/artikel/6098330]

4   Lecoq, J. and Bradby, D. (translator) (2015) *Improvisation*. p.28.

5   This 'continuum' is discussed as *is-was-will-be* by Adesola Akinleye, in her conversation with Richard Sennett on Silence and Stillness, included in this publication, pp.51-55.

6   An extract from the speech in 1920 by Millicent Fawcett, the British suffragist leader and social campaigner whose statue was placed in Parliament Square in London in 2018, following a campaign and petition by the activist Caroline Criado Perez.

CODES explores a set of non-verbal grammar rules and laws, policies and instructions encoded into the city, framing our actions and governing us often invisibly. This directly parallels dance and performance, which is notated, choreographed, codified and practiced with a broad array of techniques and technologies. In the city, our bodies have become disciplined to adhere to these codes with remarkable ubiquity. When one steps out onto the street, one has entered a space of law. Social norms around movement are codified and physically manifest in the design of the urban realm. Codes transform something abstract or ephemeral into something concrete and tangible. So, how can we challenge whose body has historically been used as standard for codifying the urban environment?

Deciphering Bodies

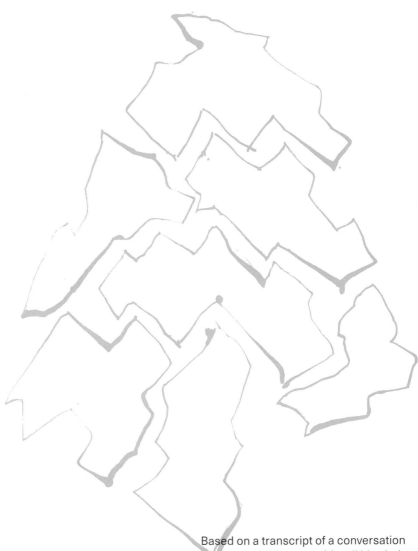

Speakers: Blanca Pujals,
Ellie Cosgrave, Fani Kostourou

Based on a transcript of a conversation
recorded for Theatrum Mundi Live in June
2020 between Blanca Pujals and Ellie
Cosgrave. The conversation was moderated
by Fani Kostourou and produced by
Andrea Cetrulo.

The project Bodily Cartographies began when I was studying architecture at the university, where we learned to design spaces based on the book *Neufert: Architect's Data*, that includes old architectural standards through anthropometric treaties of measurement. Bodily Cartographies is a research project on the relationships between the architectural anthropometric archetypes embedded into the process of design and the anthropobiometric criminologists from the 18th century. During the European Enlightenment, the new science of criminology arose following the theory of social degeneration. These criminologists created the science of anthropometrics following Quetelet's new ideas about the science of social statistics described in its treaties of man, the average man. My research examines critically their approaches to measure normalised, standardised and segregated bodies and behaviours.

F   Your project has a resonance with the work Ellie has been doing at UCL over the last years in the project Choreographing the City working with engineers, choreographers and dancers, asking how can we learn from the bodies and a choreographic thinking. Which are the main findings from this multi-disciplinary line of research, Ellie?

E

We were tasked to look at the ways that engineering needs to be transformed to make liveable cities; look at what it is about engineering thought processes, methodologies, the things that engineers value, that needs to be transformed, that will result in more liveable cities. And I came to an understanding that if we want to radically transform the way engineers think, we need to look outside, beyond the conventional approaches and discourses. For me, dance was a natural place to go to, both because I have experience as a dancer, and because I understood how connected and similar a lot of the aspirations and the approaches taken between dance makers and engineers were. Also for me, dance is a natural place where philosophy, politics and ideas around justice meet the physical world.

For this research project, we paired a choreographer and an engineer and took them out into a mobility interchange. Firstly, we asked them to document in the way they would normally document things they saw. We were interested in notation, in what they focused on, and in the frameworks through which they saw things that were important. Secondly, we asked them to talk about the possibilities for this space. We tried to avoid using the word "problem", but engineers did focus on what's wrong. Then we just asked them to explain their processes to each other, which was fascinating and really deep work that we are still unpicking from that conversation many years later.

F   In your work, choreographic thinking offers an alternative way to describe space. It suggests a critical understanding of the normalised body as a standard designated scale and measurement, through which we create the blueprint. I would like to invite you both to provide some concrete examples about this relationship between body and space so that it can become clearer what we mean exactly about this relationship and how the bodies affect the way we design and the other way around.

E

I guess the most logical place to start when thinking about cities and dance making is in mobilities. Taking two examples of the different types of scales by which engineers think about urban mobility: the first is the kind of macro scale, for example, a transport network, where there are obviously justice and rights implications about who gets to go where, what is accessible to whom, how do those networks serve socially constructed roles or different types of communities. The way engineers think about bodies in this kind of macro context reduces people to nodes with certain weights or characteristics. And engineers can make all sorts of assumptions about who these people are and what they do. I think this is where we get into your territory, Blanca, of overly rationalising human experience so that we can model it and make decisions. These reductions and rationalisations are also imbued with ideas of efficiency and practicality for economic reasons rather than justice or rights or more experience-based reasons.

That's the macro scale but clearly, we also deal with public space at a much more bodily level. I think about the way that we have designed underground stations in London, the ways that we expect people to be proximate to each other because they have got to go and earn money, and thus must get on the tube. And I am not sure if as an engineer community, we are capable of codifying the impact of the design of these spaces and I think to be able to reveal that impact would be really valuable.

B   Well, an obvious example is the hostile architecture in our cities, which we experience in everyday life, against the people living in the streets. Another case is, for example, the displacement of entire communities from their villages. In the public programme I curated in 2017, about Geographies and Forms of Power, I invited Lolita Chavez Ixcaquic, an activist from Pueblos Originarios in Guatemala, who was threatened for struggling against the toxification of their lands and the murders of their people. She explained, particularly in relation to the displacement of her community from their villages, that they were moved to concrete buildings in cities. Those buildings are designed for the standard body in the European cities, but for them, it erodes absolutely all their relationships with the land or the community. It is a form of disciplining through architecture. What I found very interesting in Ellie's work is that in architecture we are working in this kind of bodily standards of a normal body, but it is always a static body. I think it is a very powerful tool to implement movement and experience the space-time of the cities, unlike working with abstract models, with databases, numbers and mathematical bodies. Time is hardly included in these approaches; time means gatherings, relationships, sound, community and interactions, or as Karen Barad explains, intra-actions, meaning that we all emerge through affecting and being affected by each other and with all that surrounds us.

F On the one hand, there is a view that science is very much based on numbers and statistics, and on the other hand, reality is much more complex and blurred, including ideas, gestures and movements that exist both in space and time and cannot be easily quantified. So how can we get past this dualism?

E I know architecture is much better historically in incorporating arts than engineering, which does not have the language or training to engage with those topics. So, for the most part, as an industry, the conversation ends because we, as engineers, do not know what to do. And what we do as a society more generally is that we artificially separate things into dichotomies such as technical or non-technical, scientific or artistic, male or female, etc. This artificial separation results in codifying one as masculine and one as feminine; and anything that is coded masculine is better, more important and can exert power over the other. So, concepts such as care, community and identity, that are coded feminine are therefore not important, interesting, powerful or useful. The way that we've divided the world up into art or science, technology or communal care is not only incorrect, but also damaging because we hide the bits in dance making that are incredibly technical and we hide the parts in science that are incredibly personal.

B

These ideas were to construct, as you said, a form of power, a form of control. I think this is now hopefully changing, because we all know

30

that there are so many grades between these dichotomies. In this kind of technical approach to the practice, I learned a lot from Santiago Cirugeda who believes that the architect only has the tools to talk with the community and then give this expertise to them to construct their own spaces. I think it is something that we need to understand; that we are experts only with the tools, and not with the knowledge.

F   Totally, and I think, once we deconstruct these binaries the question is how does that affect city design and making? How do we design cities that can accommodate and respond effectively to different kinds of users and all kinds of possibilities?

E   It comes back to the original reason I started working with dance makers. I don't see that engineers have deeply understood what it takes to integrate some of these political and personal and embodied issues, because an integrated approach is still an alien concept in a lot of mainstream infrastructure production. You can start to re-think the design process with more reflexive ways of working. We can try to come towards engineering or infrastructure producers to translate the design process into their language; but I think we also need to sort of seduce them into more expansive ways of thinking, to be able to sit with the discomfort that comes with not being actually able to have an answer, to just understand the complexities and what they are themselves contributing to and reproducing.

B

The important thing is that we all need to be aware and critical about these issues every time we design something; this is why I talk about bodily cartographies. I remember I was very surprised by who can appear in the public space during the Extinction Rebellion movement, for example. I remember when the demonstrations happened, the black community was saying they were not allowed or preferred not to protest and demonstrate their bodies in this way because it could have been more dangerous for them if the police had arrested them.

F   It is truly alarming to see that different bodies have different powers, but also, have to rely on different kinds of infrastructures to be heard and amplify their voices. And these infrastructures, or access to them, are not the same for everyone.

Laban Score for Un-Walling the City

During the Scoring workshop organised by Theatrum Mundi at Chapelle Charbon in Paris in December 2019, we observed the inherent movement qualities in line, shape, and texture and used our own bodies to explore these qualities. By distilling the essence of these dynamic and spatial qualities from movement phrases we had improvised at the park we were able to translate them into a visual score using a form of notation known as Laban Motif Writing. We created a 'moving score' as a fluid depiction of how future park goers might connect kinesthetically and sensorially to the space through playful, spontaneous bodily movement. Our 'moving score' is a tool for embedding human physicality and embodiment into the design process.

As we walked around the site, we continued to notice layers of physical barriers such as fences, walls, and massive fragments of urban infrastructure (i.e., the peripherique) dominating the landscape. Our Laban Score for Un-Walling the City reflects upon this condition by organising the symbols in a way to suggest that movement—either bodily or architectural—can offer ways of opening up walled conditions and create moments of micro-porosity in an otherwise divided cityscape. Structured by the Laban language of movement, this score treats the symbols as graphic textures that dance across the page, activating seemingly static conditions.

This score is intended to invite movement-centred thinking that can be applied to similar conditions across the city. Thus, scoring is a means of imagining, visualising and projecting movement into a space that one is not presently inhabiting, as we did from outside the fences surrounding the site. The process of improvising scores reinforces the importance of interconnections between bodies, movement and public space at a time when many of these have been lost.

A score by Soma-City: an interdisciplinary collaboration between Rennie Tang and Lisa Sandlos, as part of their participation in the Scoring the City workshop, organised by Theatrum Mundi in December 2019 in Paris; This piece was initially published on scoring.city website.

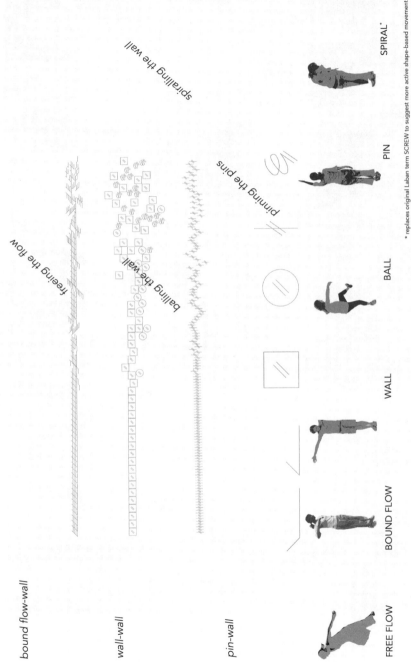

SPIRAL*

PIN

BALL

WALL

BOUND FLOW

FREE FLOW

spiralling the wall

pinning the pins

freeing the flow

balling the wall

bound flow-wall

wall-wall

pin-wall

* replaces original Laban term SCREW to suggest more active shape-based movement

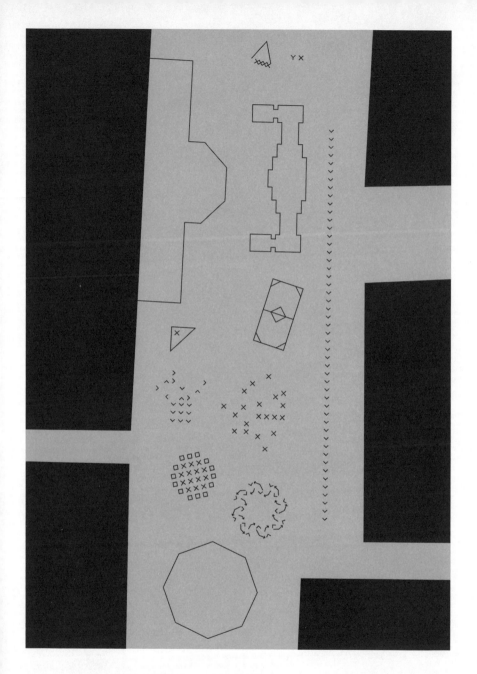

A letter/proposition by Paolo Patelli and
Giuditta Vendrame, as a new contribution
commissioned by Theatrum Mundi in
response to the theme of *Codes*.

Proposal for a New Public Sculpture

Amsterdam/Rotterdam, 2 February 2021
To the courteous attention
of Gemeente Den Haag.

With this letter, the undersigned would like to put forward a proposal for a new public sculpture in the city of The Hague. The city is host to international institutes, centres, commissions, courts, tribunals, federations, organisations, authorities, offices and embassies. The manifold jurisdictions of these entities fragment and multiply the legal space of the city. This exceptional aspect – and yet so generic – makes The Hague the ideal site for our intervention, for reasons clarified below.

The sculpture, although it won't be made out of stone, could already be called a monument. Monuments elicit through their materiality particular modes of collective memory; here, we propose to consider the motorial memory and programs. The scripts of law are drafted into our public bodies.

In their regulations, the city and its crowds are defined on the basis of a finite number of stable, isolatable and interconnected properties. Such regulations display a certain algorithmic quality; they 'discretize' human behaviour. They are sets of instructions and conditional statements, ultimately incorporating power; they are a structural force that plays into everyday life. Regulations tend to follow –or aspire to– logic and, in legal code, objects –even people– are abstracted. Humans and non-humans are known only through their predicates, their quantified qualities. Citizens, as individuals or groups, are measured in their amount: the noise they make, the age they've acquired, and the distance they keep from others.

Every day, citizens perform, on public areas, synchronized routines of elaborate moves.

Through the simple act of walking in the city, they log into a system of rules and constraints – codes that regulate and define their movements and gestures, unconscious reactions, behaviours and anticipations. The sculpture thus will stage choreographies recognised in public order acts, police acts, assembly acts, local, national and international laws that regulate behaviours and gatherings in public space.

Monuments participate in the construction of common histories and national identities, while lending their bare surfaces to counter-narratives, materialising projected consensus as much as prolonged disagreement. We do not wish to stage any specific proposition – the knowledge of a public sculpture is street wisdom – but rather the form of a particular and yet general kind of inscription: the friction of public movement on public surfaces, the physical gathering around matters of concerns, and the mundane corollary of simply walking in the city.

Choreographies of laws in space extend beyond the spectacular event to the everyday. The high visibility of the exceptional event – of the battleground – suddenly reveals the infra-ordinary in its invisibility. For example, we see in the media demonstrators who keep their march to one line, standing on the sidewalks of Washington DC. Any reading or picnic gathering of more than twenty people in one of New York City's parks requires a special event permit. In Sweden, you might need to apply for a permit to dance in public. In Cairo spontaneously discussing public matters requires a gathering of fewer than ten people.

Lines, dotted lines and physical space are the basic components of a public sculpture that aims to stage the rules that govern behaviours, transactions and gatherings. The field extends to encompass every public surface; the game is the meandering of bodies, by and despite the rules. The viewpoint from the top, and specifically from the building of the Stadhuis Den Haag on the Spui – where we suggest the monument to be installed – prescribes how, up there, one is a voyeur, a spectator. The distance from the street allows the viewer to read the city in an objectifying way, unrolling law on the territory like a map. The intertwining of daily behaviours can be maintained, if one selectively ignores some parts of the score, continually disrupting the order of the system, the law of the place. Individuals, in their daily walks and interlinked patterns, can continually transgress the stable divisions through which their subjectivity is co-opted.

A monument conceived as an annotated score imprinted on a public surface – just as the one we propose – will be a sculpture of a public choreography and although it sounds perhaps like an abstraction in formal terms, it will embody the most concrete manifestation of civic life, in the contrasting materiality of the street. It will only exist precisely and insofar as it will be performed, as a gathering, by individuals or collectives. It will be ephemeral, existing plastically only when enacted, in the presence of a participating public, including when oblivious of its involvement, captured in the flow of urban mobility.

As the 'publicness' of a space stretched between public streets and private buildings is often difficult to read the sculpture will always remain susceptible to revision and interpretation. Such ambiguity in the publicness of space derives from the non-legibility of what is public and what is private. Any space interpreted as public by someone, might be considered otherwise by someone else. A fixed and static definition of the word 'public' is impossible: publicness is always emerging and in becoming.

A composite plurality emerges from the attrition identified by the proposed intervention, from the friction between law, bodies and space, between the street and politicised bodies – including female, indigenous, of colour, queer, and more-than-human. In the last few years, we have seen collectives protesting against systemic violence and racism, dismantling symbols of colonialism in public spaces. Those collectives actualised public space. Public space, we argue, doesn't exist until it is performed, and realised through speech and deeds. No space in modern cities can be owned, managed, controlled, policed or occupied by everybody – or by nobody, for the matter. For our permanently ephemeral public sculpture, we propose to use a portion of the space owned and managed by the City. The sculpture will describe a set of overlapping rules, derived from local and national laws. It will be composed of fifteen diagrams, traced on a field of multi-coloured acrylic lines – Road Liner – occupying a surface of 30m × 15m. The paint used will become part of the accumulation of visual layers in the cityscape of The Hague, soliciting vectors for movement, set in time and space.

Law is designed and made, and it is almost infinitely malleable. The proposed public art project will make explicit the often-implicit regulations defining the types and levels of use of public space – e.g., how many can gather without a permit. By doing so, it will contribute to choreographing new forms of civic and aesthetic engagement with hidden or abstract layers of the city. If it doesn't provide an operating manual, it will present itself as a score for a modern dance.

Attached is the blueprint of the permanently ephemeral public sculpture for the city of The Hague. We hope you will consider our proposal and we look forward to receiving your thoughts.

Paolo Patelli
Giuditta Vendrame

FLUX focuses on how the city is in a constant state of change, continually evolving and redefining itself through the bodies and the lived experiences of its inhabitants. It tackles passive interpretations of notions such as stillness, absence and presence, and suggests framing them in relation to bodily awareness in the city. Our ability to know and self-construct the image of the city is forever in flux. We make the city and the city continually makes us. We do not exist in isolation: The city connects to the micro-level of human and non-human actors and the macro-level of the global stage, and within this, our bodies and movement contribute to the continual ebb and flow of city life. Being in the city and being in space takes effort. But what does it mean to be in the city? How can we resist movement and celebrate the quieter spectrum of motion?

The Sense of Presence

How is the sense of presence – so important in performing well onstage – felt, seen or created in the city? American ballet choreographer George Balanchine defines presence as the feeling of being 'right here, right now!' How can that liveliness be achieved in a city? Most of the current architecture and planning practices create life-less and inert environments. Artists and culture makers have to struggle to rouse people from such environments. We are mindful that presence is not politically innocent: a looming crowd evokes the feeling of being present at something important, and, in another dimension, presence and liveliness can be repressed by the authorities or by the sanctions of tenancy and ownership.

Time is one of the four dimensions, along with knowledge, materials and place, to explore the sense of presence in terms of when, how, what and where. Time is an enduring concept in architecture and urban studies. Lewis Mumford, an American historian, sociologist and critic wrote that the city makes time visible.[1] It becomes visible in the context and condition of performance. Recently, there has been a re-emergence of the notion of the temporary, pop-up, meanwhile or interim use, that offers a more flexible, more variable, and more 'democratic' space for culture in the city. Some of this, however, might be due to neoliberal changes, meaning that funding and spatial constraints align with an elevated social burden on the arts and cultural practices to be more nimble, more engaged, and yet much more precarious. While, the large, costly and bureaucratically heavy legacy of cultural organisations and institutions still preoccupy the cultural landscape and are being reproduced in global circuits of cultural policy that favours expensive, permanent icons. But what would a shift to the temporary mean for architecture? Is the division of temporary versus distinctive a false one? Can temporary structures, performances or events in the city translate into legacies of knowledge and relationship? How do we negotiate time? Can the temporary leave a trace?

1   Mumford, L. (1938) *The Culture of Cities.*

A thought piece published by Theatrum Mundi in June 2013, in relation to the *Negotiating Spaces* salon series – a nine-month investigation on themes emerging from a year of collaborative workshops with artists, urbanists and scholars in London, New York, Frankfurt and Copenhagen.

Negotiating Time:
Can the temporary leave a trace?

Choreography is a good wrestler with the question: can the temporary leave a trace? Among my projects [in 2013] this knack that choreography has is perhaps most evident in my adaptation of a solo choreographic score that I commissioned from the choreographer Deborah Hay, a leading figure in post-modern dance. In this unique annual project, designed by Hay fourteen years ago, she invited up to twenty experienced choreographer/performers to commission her to create a solo score. We worked together as a group for ten days to learn the score under Hay's direction, before each going our separate ways to independently begin the process of creating our own adaptation of it, by practicing the score once a day, five days a week, for a minimum of nine months, before it was performed publicly.

In Hay's work, the choreographic score takes the form of a highly specific use of written language that triggers the performance but is not prescriptive of precise movement outcomes. She writes the score in such a way that it is not possible to give it a singularly permanent, wholly repeatable manifestation. The score can only be performed by engaging in a negotiation between the landscape that it defines and the performer's constantly unfolding perception within it.

Through daily practice, the architecture of the score evolves an increasingly tangible identity, while at the same time always remaining un-fixed. Dance artist Rachel Krische has said of her own experience of this work, that it is a practice of 'drawing a line in pencil with one hand, while at the same time continually rubbing it out with the other'. The performer is always making the trace, but keeping it temporary; establishing a pattern while also unpatterning it; creating a travelling horizon that sustains a space of possibility between the patterning and the unpatterning.

That space is important because it offers the possibility to exercise agency. Although my body, brain and mind could not begin to function in the world without the profound support of my habitual, familiar patterns of action, the automaticity of those deeply embedded patterns distances me from my capacity to consciously choose how or when those patterns are triggered. In order to exercise choice, I need to actively and continually re-awaken my awareness of the habitual and dissociate my action from it. Only then, within that temporary space, does it become possible for me to re-direct my action along other paths.

A reflection by Matthias Sperling as part of his participation in the *Negotiating Time* salon which took place at the SHED, The National Theatre in London; initially published in *Beyond the Public* by Theatrum Mundi in 2014

Engineers can learn a lot from dance when designing transport

There is little more important for the sustainability of cities than the ways we move around them. With transportation estimated to account for thirty per cent of energy consumption across the majority of the world's most developed nations, reducing the necessity for energy-reliant vehicles is fundamental to addressing the environmental impact of mobility.

But as cities become the predominant habitat[1] for most people in the world, it is important to think about other kinds of sustainability of cities too. The ways we travel impact our physical and mental health, our social lives, our access to work and culture, and the air we breathe. Engineers are tasked with changing how we travel around cities through urban design, but the engineering industry still rests on the assumptions that have led to the creation of the energy-consuming transport systems we have now: the emphasis placed solely on efficiency, speed and quantitative data. We need new approaches in order to help engineers create the radical changes required to make moving around cities healthier, more enjoyable and less environmentally damaging. Dance might hold some of the answers. That is not to suggest everyone should dance their way to work, however healthy and happy it might make us. But rather that the techniques used by choreographers to experiment with and design movement in dance could offer engineers with tools to stimulate new ideas in city-making.

Sociological theory about the nature of work can help us to understand why choreography can help. Richard Sennett, an influential urbanist and sociologist who transformed ideas about the way cities are made, argues that urban design – including, we would argue, engineering and planning as much as it does architecture – has suffered from a severance between mind and body since the advent of the architectural blueprint; whereas the medieval builders improvised and adapted construction through their intimate knowledge of materials and embodied experience of the conditions in a site.[2] Building designs are now conceived and stored in media technologies that detach the designer from the physical and social realities they are creating. The 'disembodied design practices' created by these technologies are essential for managing the technical complexity of the modern city, but they simplify reality in the process.

To illustrate, Sennett discusses the Peachtree Center in Atlanta, a development emblematic of the modernist approach to urban planning prevalent in the 1970s. Peachtree created a grid of streets and towers intended as a new pedestrian-friendly downtown for Atlanta. This, according to Sennett, failed because its designers had invested too much faith in computer-aided design to tell them how it would operate. The designers didn't understand that purpose-built street cafes could not operate in the hot sun without the awnings, common in older buildings, and would need energy-consuming air conditioning instead; or that its giant car park would feel so desolate as to put people off from getting out of their cars. What seems entirely predictable and

A thought piece by John Bingham-Hall, initially published on theconversation.com in October 2017.

controllable on screen has unexpected results when translated into reality. The same is true in transport engineering, which uses models to predict and shape the way people move through the city. Again, these models are necessary, but they are built on specific worldviews, in which certain assumed forms of efficiency and safety are privileged over other embodied experiences of the city. Designs that seem logical in models appear counterintuitive in the embodied experience of their users.

The guard rails that are familiar to anyone having attempted to cross a British road, for example, were an engineering solution to pedestrian safety based on models that prioritise the smooth flow of traffic, guiding pedestrians to specific crossing points and slowing them down through staggered access points. In doing so, they make crossings feel longer, introducing psychological barriers[3] greatly impacting those that are the least mobile, and encouraging some others to make dangerous crossings to get around them. These barriers don't just make it harder to cross the road, they sever communities and decrease opportunities for healthy transport. As a result, many are now being removed,[4] causing disruption and increasing costs and waste.

In order to bring about fundamental changes to the ways we use our cities, engineering will need to develop a richer understanding of what motivates people to move in certain ways, and how it affects them. Choreography may not seem an obvious choice for tackling this problem. Yet it shares the aim of designing patterns of movement within spatial constraints. Choreography is an embodied art form developed almost entirely through instant feedback between improvisation of ideas with the body, and tactile feedback from those ideas. It uses models and forms of notation to plan movements that dancers will make, with

qualitative as well as quantitative information. Choreographers have an extremely rich understanding of the psychological, aesthetic and physical implications of different ways of moving. Observing the choreographer Wayne McGregor, cognitive scientist David Kirsh described how he 'thinks with the body'.[5] Kirsh argues that by using the body to simulate outcomes, McGregor is able to imagine solutions that would not be possible using purely abstract thought. This kind of embodied knowledge is given great value in many realms of expertise, but currently has no place in formal engineering design processes.

What if transport engineers were to improvise design solutions and get instant feedback about how they would work from their own embodied experience? What if they could model designs at full scale in the way choreographers experiment with groups of dancers? What if they designed for emotional as well as functional effects? By comparing the techniques and worldviews of choreography and engineering, we aim to find out.[6]

1   Collyer, M. (2015), "The world's urban population is growing – so how can cities plan for migrants?", *THE CONVERSATION* [https://theconversation.com/the-worlds-urban-population-is-growing-so-how-can-cities-plan-for-migrants-49931]
2   Sennett, R. (2009) *The Craftsman.*
3   Orr, D. (2010) "Street Pride Briefing 4: Guard rails", *Civic Voice* [http://www.civicvoice.org.uk/uploads/files/Briefing_note_4_Guard_rails_-_Final.pdf]
4   Transport For London (2009), "Guardrail removal programme" [http://content.tfl.gov.uk/Item09-Guardrail-Removal-Programme.pdf]
5   Kirsh, D. (2010) "Thinking with the body", *The 32nd Annual Conference of the Cognitive Science Society* [http://adrenaline.ucsd.edu/Kirsh/Articles/Interaction/thinkingwithbody.pdf]
6   This refers to the ongoing research project, Choreographing the City, a collaboration between UCL Urban Innovation and Infrastructure and Theatrum Mundi.

Connective Scores for Humans and Non-Humans

Find yourself somewhere outside your house. It might be in the tube, on a street or a plaza, in a library, an office, or an elevator.

1   The place of your choice has the possibility to have other lives within, human and non-human.

2   Remember that non-human lives might be invisible to your eyes but there they are! (birds, insects, bacteria, micro-organisms...)

3   You can repeat the following scores as much as you want, share them with others, experiment and have fun!

A score by Pepa Ubera, as a new contribution commissioned by Theatrum Mundi in response to the theme of *Flux*.

HUMAN TO HUMAN
Caring for strangers

Somehow you have found yourself in stillness (or an idea of it), perhaps you are seated. Or holding a bar to support yourself. Did you choose to be in the tube?

Notice if there are other bodies in the space! You first see them with your eyes. Now, without looking at them, can you imagine how their body weight is relaxing into the environment? It might be a surface, a seat, a wall? Can you sense their breaths moving, the edges of their bodies blurring in the atmosphere...?

Close your eyes for 30 seconds and imagine the space that is between you and the other bodies. Try to imagine some colour or texture of that in-between space, that distance...

take your time

Choose a part of your body other than your hand and then imagine the length of the space that could connect that part to another part of a human body. Meanwhile, notice your breathing and the connection of your feet to the ground. Can you choose to connect with someone that seems quite different to you?

Close your eyes! Extend your perception towards them, count 10 seconds to make this happen.

take your time

If you could choose an action to show you care for the stranger(s) with whom you have just connected, what would that be? Caressing the head? Sitting closer? Or just listening to their breathing? Now, we could also use our emphatic imagination to do this, can you sense this empathy emanating from your chest? Or even the back of your neck? Whatever action you choose, notice how your body opens up into the space. One more time to make it happen.

take your time

The next score involves more than human bodies and you might like to refresh yourself, maybe have a walk before you start, or wander around. Can you lie down on the floor? Drink some water...

The next score involves more than human bodies and you might like to refresh yourself, maybe have a walk before you start, or wander around. Can you lie down on the floor? Drink some water...

HUMAN TO NON-HUMAN
Relationships that come to the surface

Routes of transmission – becoming invisible to let others appear.

Have a few deep breaths; inhale and exhale deeply. It could get tiring and wild to imagine so much! So please don't feel you have to engage with all the scores in one go. Do as you please and notice if you need breaks.

Now, in order to connect with non-human entities, you might need to quieten down your inner voice, your thoughts, soften your gaze. Choose a plant, an animal, or a body of water to connect with. Or perhaps go on imagining the microorganisms that are not visible to the human eye but that you know are there in space.

Turning. This time choose to connect with these entities with the whole body, turning towards them and away from them, transforming the back of your body to the front, giving them equal presence. As you keep turning, notice how the other non-human entities are turning too; the movement might be completely invisible to your eyes but not to your imagination. You might also try to twist your torso and head side to side turning like a sunflower towards the sun.

What is this relation becoming?
Could you imagine other people doing the same practice at the same time?

take your time

ONENESS
Environment, Human and Non-Human , Flocking

Now you are connecting with the environment and non-human entities in a multidimensional way. Flocking like birds, move together, wait to see who is leading the way, share leadership as you move along.

The space you are inhabiting might start giving you hints of what to do next, then the plant, the animal or the sea (the non-human sentient) will initiate the next movement for you to follow suit; continue with this dance of awareness until you feel one with all.

take your time

CONTINGENCIES gets its inspiration from the principle of improvisation in dance-making. Being contingent means to focus on a future event or circumstance, which is possible but cannot be predicted with certainty. It asks how city-making can be conceived as a means of speculating about how things could be, to imagine possible futures. This is not the usual sort of prediction, forecasting or computer modelling that built environment profes-sionals engage in. Instead, contingency is concerned with 'what if' questions and how they could open up debates and dis-cussions around the kind of future people want – or do not want. It asks professionals to consider how they can learn from other disciplines to shift the paradigm in the way they conceive space, place and the urban realm. How might they provide and accommodate for the contingent?

Silence and Stillness

Speakers: Adesola Akinleye
and Richard Sennett

Based on a transcript of a conversation
recorded for Theatrum Mundi Live in
October 2020 between Adesola Akinleye
and Richard Sennett. The podcast was
produced by Andrea Cetrulo.

A   During the conversations I had with architects and engineers, there was this idea of stillness not as a lack of movement but as lack of capturing of *nowness*, the kind of being present. Presence in relation to absence. This idea connects us to music and four concepts in relationship with each other: stillness, silence, absence and presence. And these are significant in terms of how people can feel they are part of the city they are in.

R

Stillness and silence are mediated in music by rhythm, and there are pieces of music in which the notion of beats, that marks rhythm, begins to disappear. It is a relationship between steadily beating time and a kind of slowness which almost faces the beat. The most interesting thing about it is that moving towards stillness, being absolutely immobile but present; it is a moment that also happens in cities in a kind of ordinary way, in just sitting in a café and watching people in the street. We are not aware of the passing of time. That's something very difficult for us to do in music.

Curiously the piece in which nothing happens and there is no beat tends to tune the audience much more to the ambient sounds around them. The audience begins to hear more because musicians are present on stage but doing nothing. They create a song that is missing, and that is absence; when you have musicians sitting but not moving at all. When you look at the stage and see this huge dressed platform, that I would not say is absence, that is a stillness which makes sure we are looking for other presences.

My question to you Adesola, as a dancer, is how the things I explained in music happens in dancing. And the question for both of us is: what are people experiencing in cities when they are simply present, not doing anything, and nothing is expected to be done?

A   There is a sense of intention involved in what we are discussing. When you dance, there is a sort of *nowness* that I am thinking of as *is-was-will-be;* a kind of *continuum* in John Dewey's pragmatic theory. Things that are connected. And absence is the intention of having no continuation to the past or future.

R

One of the basic elements of presence in music is called *air pause*. That is a slight separation between strict rhythm, between one beat and next. Every singer does it. We do it in speech. It is something that we have to learn to do very carefully in music in order to make it phrased. If I am playing something that begins in the middle of a beat, I have to make just a slightest pause – if it is in 4, between 2 and 3 – to indicate that we're going to do something new. And that's how we make a presence. We begin to store time in this very subtle way. That's why a lot of instrumental players are so interested in studying singing because even if they're not using their throats, what singers do to shape those with their voice, in sound we have to do with bowing, and with some instruments sometimes with alternative fingerings. Things that mark a slight suspension of time. It is a really important way of making something present. I don't know if there is any kind of urban reverberation to that.

A   As part of my *is-was-will-be* I want to highlight that time is going to be interrupted and there needs to be an establishment of its ordering to be interrupted, that's the idea of continuum. Some people don't have that connection to the place they are present in, or their presence hasn't been calculated. Their presence in the moment is there, but their sense of being part of a continuum of that place is not as strong as in other people. So, their ability to play with that rhythm to interrupt or to have that moment to happen is limited because they are not part of the continuum in the first place.

R

Let's explore this further. If you are in a space and everything you do is smoothed in that space, you are not really present. It always has to be some little process of disrupting in your static presence. I don't think the continuum is the right way to mark that presence, but rather that disruption.

A   How about thinking of the idea of continuum, not as something smooth, but as melody, as something that has a pattern that you move through and in, having no rhythm, no underlying thread playing in and out or interrupting? You find yourself part of a pattern weaving in and out of, and one can feed into it without any interruption, as a sense of a continuum.

R

For a musician, there is a difference between what's written and what's performed. If it is possible that you perform exactly what was written down, you would be bored. You begin to riff, on classical music as much as in jazz, what is written down; the continuous is the score. There is so much interpretative work going on to create that sense, which is off the page, all sorts of innovative and technical things feeding to the notion that something is being done to the score. So, this is my obsession: how we, in any of our achieved presence, resist doing what would be normal and putting ourselves into it.

A   If we think of the score as the continuum, then maybe stillness and silence are very good tools of resistance. If the score is a kind of written pattern, how you interrupt that flow is through where you improvise, where silence and stillness is, or where to extend them or add to them.

R

Right. How would it work for you as a dancer?

A   As I am dancing, it's the same thing – as you have described in music. There is a kind of rhythm that you're keeping with your body and you are all the time playing with that. So you might be holding something a tiny bit longer and bringing out quicker, again more slowly, so there is always this kind of self-interpretation or pushing the edges of the score, the rhythm of the exercise or the piece of the choreography. I think that's quite an exciting idea because if stillness and silence are tools of resistance – resistance as a kind of rapping of how we know we are alive – then they become much less empty or passive and much more active.

R

Right. You are not reading something; you are enacting it. I am curious about choreography and classical dance. In ballet you have something that is equivalent to a score. How do you resist that score?

A   In ballet, you might have a variation as a set of movements that you're doing, and each time you do it, it would be different because you're responding to the moment differently. It's never the same thing and I'm sure it's the same in music. Although you know what the steps are, they're never the same thing repeated.

R

Do you have an idea of correctness in ballet? When a step is performed as it should be?

A   The correctness is in the technique. For me, technique is about how you have the freedom to interpret the score. So, the technique holds you from hurting yourself and gives you the ability to then play with the variation. So, the correctness comes to having the technique to be able to play, the tools that you are using to express this play or interact with the score or the choreography. So, when you see a dancer that has beautifully done that and it touches you, it is because the technique is there, and you trust that this person can play with stillness and silence, or the frictions of the flow, you can see it in their body. Then you can be with them in this resistance, and that's the exciting part, that's where the artistry is. In modified contemporary dance, the same as ballet, the technique is about the intention of what you do. You are able to physically explore the things that you started with the intention of doing and technique gives you the tool for that. I am imagining the score or choreography almost like a piece of lace that has all these kinds of patterns and holes, with all the possibilities of threading through many different roots even though you're within the same lace.

R

That's nice. Maybe in that way there is a kind of difference between, let's say, improvised dance and jazz. Most jazz improvisations – so-called free jazz – follow a set of prohibitions about what not to do. You can find that even in young jazz players today. Basically, they're avoiding doing certain things that would be closing off. Prohibitions like "don't go there" or "don't make that shift". Maybe that doesn't exist with the dance the same way. You are not thinking "what not to do", are you?

A   In dance you could find a very similar thing. It's a prohibition of where you can put your weight. If you think about all dance as a way of shifting your weight through your body; it's like playing with gravity, using your muscles and physicality of your body. The more codified, the more you have ways of playing around your weight and gravity. When you are using a form of dance that draws more on improvised techniques then there is this idea of prohibition – even the idea of battling and Break Dancing – there is a certain close-ness with the other dancer. All of those are about where to put your weight, some spaces that are prohibited, almost touching that thing and then almost moving away from it. Part of it is like jazz music, the indication of "I could have gone there but I didn't".

R

That's resistance. The anchors for us as modern performers are "don't go there and don't do that" rather than "this is how to do it". And there is a pleasure of breaking the prohibition and playing that forbidden chord.

A   Let's move back to the idea of urban design and cities. If we are in a creative time of prohibition that as an artist you can play with, and it's something exciting, it is the feeling that people have when they're in their everyday life. So, I wonder if our relationship with the rules is to see them as a lace, to play in and out of, is that how the average experience on the street is? Or is the lace like a piece that doesn't appear to be playable with?

R

This embodied relationship with the city raises a big problem in our dialogue about art and society, as disembodied dialogue. This is Theatrum Mundi's aim to show how to rethink that relationship between embodiment and design. My prescience about this is that architects will never get there, particularly those who design on the computer. They don't make an interactive dialogue for what they build. Urban design is so imprisoned by what seems to be functional and requisite, where the score is absolute and this kind of embodiment is very difficult. Most urban spaces do not have any quality of what we are talking about.

Dancing in the Streets

The immediate and emergent crises faced by the contemporary city demand a trans-disciplinary approach; one that connects and collaborates across distant and seemingly unconnected fields, sharing and challenging ideas, methods and solutions. Each diverse and invested field of expertise has its role to play in bringing into existence a more emancipatory city; one that is sympathetic and intuitive towards the diverse movements and heterogeneous needs of its citizenry.

Cities, citizens, cultures and ideas are in a permanent state of flux. Whether the acceleration of urban transport infrastructures across continents, the movement of migrating people across national borders, or the reserve armies of labour that traverse from the peripheries to the centres of cities each day, the contemporary city must be defined by its relationship to movement.

As such, much of engineering's creative responsibility is concerned with how to maximise and make more efficient the many infrastructural networks and mechanisms that facilitate the everyday movement of people – and commodities – in and through the urban landscape. This central mobility-problem already has emergent tensions. An understanding of urban transport contains a quantitative logic: increasing the speed and quantities of transport services, whilst reducing costs and maximising the positive economic impact on the benefitting industries. In some respects, the contra-

dictions of the mobility-problem present themselves to engineers as a set of problems and puzzles. Which in turn presents the engineer with the opportunity to use the language, logic and epistemology of engineering to provide concurrent answers. For engineers, their Cartesian dualism is the balance of problem and solution. There is also an entirely different lens through which the urban mobility-problem can be considered. Namely, understanding the transport network from a qualitative perspective, and seeking to fundamentally understand urban space and urban transport from the perspective of experience: do I feel safe? Is this train comfortable? Does this bus accommodate for disabled access? By focusing on human experience, it is radical to invert politics and economics playing out across transport infrastructures. Taking as a starting point the infinite micro-interactions between bodies, transport networks and cities, we can begin to understand the urban mobility-problem from the perspective of the everyday. This challenge to quantitatively-considered urban politics suggests that the city itself does not exist singularly at the macro levels of politics and economics, but instead is made and remade each day by the citizens who constitute it.

Being a part of such an expansive and productive urban transport machine has a direct psychological impact on each user, whilst also contributing to a wider mobility culture across the city – do we live in a city where we are encouraged to explore, or to commute? Do we live in a city that has isolated areas, that is unsafe or unaffordable to traverse? Transport is perhaps the greatest democratic mechanism within the city. It allows for the emancipatory qualities of urban life; the Bermanian right to reinvent

A thought piece by Luke Gregory-Jones as part of his participation in the Improvisatory Design workshop led by Ellie Cosgrave, John Bingham-Hall and Hagit Yakira in August 2018 at UCL's Pedestrian Accessibility Movement Environment Laboratory (PAMELA).

yourself and create new and dynamic social bodies; 'to go on endlessly creating the world anew';[1] to be accessed and savoured by all, independent of the barriers of class, gender, sexuality or race. Transport can be the great egalitarian leveller. But this liberalising infrastructure is predicated on a type of network and culture that maximises accessibility – in its quantitative but also qualitative forms.

Choreographing the City project led by Ellie Cosgrave at UCL STEaPP and John Bingham-Hall at Theatrum Mundi thus invited practitioners from both choreography and engineering to participate in a workshop that sought to explore choreographic ways of designing urban mobility. The intention of the research was to create a new discourse – directly between active practitioners of choreography and urban engineering – that, firstly, uncovered the fundamental logics of each discipline, and secondly exposed the latent possibilities of collaborative action.

This workshop, organised in June 2018, followed five initial research interviews each pairing one choreographer and one expert in urban transport. These pairings were then invited into a space that embodied the urban mobility-problem, within which the participants were asked to complete two tasks: firstly, to describe the space and secondly to plan an intervention into the space. The intention of these two tasks was to expose the three fundamental phases or moments of creative production: firstly, epistemology and knowledge gathering, then the act of design itself, and finally the assessment process. This format was also self-reflexive, offering the participants the opportunity to reflect on their interpretation and performance of the tasks, and also in turn offering broader and more phenomenological analysis of their discipline and industry.

Five categories of analysis presented themselves as self-evident within the research:

Description, Agency, Modelling, Design and Assessment. These categories, present throughout each of the workshops and interviews, provided fundamental insight into the real-world workings of both disciplines, and also each one of them pointed towards the latent possibilities of collaborative action. For instance, engineering modelling – as we learnt – is limited and curtailed by impending deadlines, budgetary restrictions and an over-reliance on the unquestionable validity of computer simulation. Choreographing the City seeks to challenge the singular pre-eminence of computational modelling in favour of human-scale modelling for the broadest, most qualitative understanding of the human body, human movement and human experience.

However, within the epistemological framework of engineering – namely the dualism of problem-solution – there is little scope given to allowing design to be guided by experiential, affective and qualitative intentions. This therefore raises the imminent question: what would urban transport be if it was specifically designed to enhance and enrich human experience? And, following on, what impact could this have on the (mobility) culture of a city?

To bring to the surface these real and latent possibilities, the choreographer Hagit Yakira was invited to, as part of the project If One Keeps Walking, undertake a series of choreographed promenade performances to stretch the boundaries between the everyday action of walking and the artistry of dancing. How might the spaces travelled through be redesigned around expanded modes of movement? In addition to drawing attention to the values assumed in urban engineering, what are the other potentials of improvisatory movement as a technique within design processes? How do the design assumptions about the kind of movement that can be engineered, change when the design process is the outcome itself?

Improvisatory Design

To improvise is to create form spontaneously, whose only purpose is often its own existence, although improvisation always takes place within certain parameters. Engineering requires improvisation but is framed as a goal-driven process formed of rational steps.

The first part of Yakira's improvisatory workshop, which took place in the UCL lab, focused on movement. She was able to isolate the issue of speed – an issue endemic to the urban mobility-problem – and explore alternative modes of movement guided by different rhythms and values. The participants were asked to slow down and then speed up, to walk close together and then far apart. The conditions of experience inherent to commuting or riding a bus were recreated, and then transformed into a plastic, malleable experience that the participants – or as Yakira insisted, 'authors' – were able to control.

Yakira then led the participants outside the stage into the world. She led a walk focusing on different elements of travel that challenge the dominance of forward motion: slowing down and speeding up, stopping, connecting, interacting and watching. Yakira once again introduced basic movement rules, limiting speeds and interactions, whilst allowing for a different experience of moving through urban space. The participants were exploring notions of speed and mobility across roads and pavements, navigating parked and moving cars as well as pedestrians and cyclists. They experimented with two ways of creating form through improvisation: firstly, building a space around an improvised set of movements and secondly, moving within an improvised space. This workshop intended to open up and explore the politics of urban mobility; how movement through a city doesn't have to be choreographed by the logic of commuting, but instead can point to a more interactive, more sympathetic, human experience.

For Yakira, the creation of the choreographic work, as with the movement workshop, follows an open-ended process that allows for form to arise from improvisation. This process-led approach is, in many ways, the diametric inversion of the engineering dualism of problem-solution. This specific and targeted workshop concerning choreographic modelling reflected on the emergent themes, particularly modelling as the essential connection between the original epistemological act of gathering knowledge about the world-as-it-is and the design of an intervention into it.

Yakira's improvisatory design workshop shows choreography's role in challenging the dominant values, rhythms and shapes of movement within the city as well as narrow definitions of human actors in computational simulation. This form of modelling plays out at a human scale, allowing real and genuine human interaction to guide the creative process. Such a trans-disciplinary approach brings together the full tapestry of interested disciplines and expertise, and intends to create a city that is more attuned and sympathetic to its citizenry, and specifically for the urban transport network to play a central and liberational role in the unfolding of urban freedoms.

1   Berman, M. (2020) *All That Is Solid Melts Into Air.*
P. 288.

The Act of Loitering

Being contingent is an approach to challenge the spatial codes, societal and cultural constructs that dictate and limit our public behaviour and ways of *being* and *belonging* in the city. I argue that *contingency*, as a form of resistance, can be practised through collaborative performance; as a way to expose the production of meaning and value systems; as a tool to hack, critique and challenge them; to transform us from bystanders into active citizens.[1] Performance, therefore, is crucial to the fabric of urban life as a mechanism for collective identity to be played out in the public realm.

Performance is a Process

Whilst performance in its traditional theatrical sense is often the end product, I believe that when intersected with urbanism and architecture, performativity becomes a form of research in its own right, a work in process or a contingent exploration. In the same vein being propositional within the world of architecture does not always necessitate a built form. The act of performance, movement and inhabitation have the power to transform spaces across the city. Contingency, through performance, can offer new realities or plausible utopias that can meaningfully contribute to a sense of belonging in the city.

In my emerging practice, I use performance as a tool to provoke and speculate on possible urban futures, centring on the notion of contingency – even lingering –

A proposition by Rebecca Faulkner, as a new contribution commissioned by Theatrum Mundi in response to the theme of *Contingencies*.

as it is often deemed problematic in public space. Through collaboration with dancers or 'movement workers', I understand how our bodies can be used as tools to critique the ways spatial conditions in the public realm are designed. The collaborative performative work I make is underpinned by personal experience of being in the city, emotional and bodily responses to spatial or social scenarios and an understanding of the critical, theoretical and historical situation that have produced these. When these elements merge, performance can become charged – the actions we impose, if numerable enough, have the potential to meaningfully transform the world. This thought piece reflects on the publicly staged performance, *The Act of Loitering: A City Awakening,* which sought to celebrate the quieter spectrum of movement; stillness. It stemmed from my ongoing research into how spatial codes and legacies dictate public behaviour and how this has almost invisibly framed my own experiences of city life, specifically as a woman in the public realm.

There is no single way of knowing the city,[2] and each of our experiences is different, but I know that being in the city takes effort. As I move through the city, I am constantly changing how I occupy space – how small or big I make myself, how known or concealed I make my presence. This is a scenario that is not limited to women, but for the purposes of this thought-piece I will be specifically looking through the female lens. Liz Kelly and Fiona Vera-Gray's[3] argument that 'avoiding certain behaviour directed towards women has required strategies and planning' resonates with me. The authors ask us to 'go beyond simply looking at what happens to women' in the public realm, and to broaden our understandings of how women (and girls) respond to those scenarios' and unpack the historical context that has created them. *The Act of Loitering* was the culmination of looking at the city through three lenses: the aforementioned personal experiences of presence in the city; previous performative work exploring instructions and rules encoded into the built environment; and understanding the historical legacy of how women were depicted and governed in public and private settings in eighteenth and early nineteenth century England.[4]

In the early 1800s, female presence and mobility in the city was of great public concern. Magazines of the time simultaneously encouraged women to take suitable exercise whilst regulating their movement, advising walking 'in certain ways, at certain times and with a companion'.[5] Accompanying my walking-based explorations of the city for *The Act of Loitering* was Rebecca Solnit's *Wanderlust: A History Of Walking*.[6] The chapter on "Walking After Midnight" presents how in the same historical era, to be seen alone, walking in the city created the assumption that a woman was sexually available.[7]

Vagrancy or 'wandering without apparent resources or purpose—was and sometimes still is a crime.'[8] Through the 1800s, the introduction of 'Vagrancy Acts' – amongst many limits on civil liberties – furthered the control of female urban movement in a complex and codified manner, underpinning the societal construct of respectable women in public space and their counterpart, *public women*, those who dwelled in the private sphere of the home. The Vagrancy Act of 1822 was the first use of *Night Walkers* as a synonym for prostitution, defined as idle or 'disorderly persons wandering in public street.'[9] The 1824 amendments expanded the public realm to any place of public resort. Solnit remarks how 'the law makes it virtually impossible to be a respected public female

figure, and ever since, women's sexuality has been public business,'[10] a sentiment that sadly rings true.

Though much feminist work has been achieved in indoor settings, it is my understanding that the historic and many more contemporary laws still dictate female urban movement today, which *The Act of Loitering* sought to challenge.

Loitering is a funny term. It is both passive and active, a construct of space and time. It means many things to different people; to some, it may summon imagery of soliciting, to others it may be synonymous with youths hanging about and causing a nuisance and for some, it may instil a sense of fear. Most likely, as an action, it conjures up negative connotations. Put simply, loitering is an act of dwelling/staying/being in a public space for a protracted period, without any apparent purpose.[11] This definition is purposefully vague, relying on discretion to determine both the accepted length of time and intent behind people's presence in the public realm. Presence in the city becomes loitering once policed,[12] instructing us where we can be and for how long. These instructions are codified through personnel, hostile street objects that limit or restrict access, signs that prohibit congregating, or through surveillance technology such as CCTV cameras. Loitering, therefore, cannot be divorced from privilege, permission and human bias, the effects of which are never felt equally. Across the city, you will be constantly reminded: no loitering!

The Act of Loitering was the climactic moment of a series of improvised choreographed performances over six months. The enactments scaled up from the size of an A4 paper to the size of the city – almost. It was staged successively in three parts of London, across three sites or instances of the city with varying levels of publicness.

Performing *Loitering* was a strange kind of rehearsal for a future where loitering and lingering are celebrated, protected and enacted across the city. But, what does it mean *to act*? The term *act* means taking *action*; *doing something*, or *behaving in a way specified* or even *performing*. It can also mean *a thing done; a deed*, a *criminal act* or a *pretence*, whilst also *being a written law passed by Parliament*. Therefore, *act*, in the context of this performance, is applicable on many levels.

The first selected site was the intersection of Rosebery Avenue and Warner Street, a CCTV blind-spot and the point at which my privilege was called into question during a previous performance. Two off-duty officers stopped me and asked if I had a 'permit' for marking the floor with chalk, as it was technically 'criminal damage'. The second selected site was the Barbican estate, owned by The City of London Corporation, and originally built as a 'gift to the nation'. Paradoxically it borders the 'Traffic and Environmental Zone', commonly known as the *ring of steel,* which uses patterns of old London to redraw 'a new urban plan that is easy to police [generating] anonymous non-places [...] that discourage [...] lingering.'[13] And the final site, The South Bank, is a commonly used pubic realm bordering galleries and theatres and serves as a place for gathering. Ironically, it somehow felt the most public despite its 'Privately Owned Public Space' status and heavy use of CCTV cameras. On reflection more variety of instances of the city may have been fruitful.

Each site was also selected for its stepped levels and framing, offering axial views to monitor and survey the enactments below. Responding to a public open call, I was assisted by Silvia, Jackie and Kanel, three female dancers with an embodied knowledge of movement. Together we explored through a one-day performance what it meant to occupy space in the city. *The Act of Loitering* was grounded in improvisation, the limited briefing allowed the dancers to move in a non-choreographed manner, and could be seen as a rehearsal for occupying a piece of the public realm and the permission to do so. The performance, although fleeting, offered a glimpse into a plausible utopia where loitering, stillness and presence are celebrated.

Performed on International Women's Day 2020, sandbags – a fascination of mine – were reimagined as performative, tethered props. Giant, wearable versions were fabricated and tethered to constrain and liberate, with their heavy nature restraining my collaborators' bodies, momentarily gifting loitering. Witnessing three women lumber giant sandbags across sites in London may at first seem ludicrous, and in the words of one private security guard, "bizarre". Long after we were gone, the trace of this performance remained, in the memories of those accidental audience members and in the dust we left, the mix of sand and chalk spilt onto the streets.

In an ideal world, this would be a call to loiter, to collectively take action and get out into the street, to claim back and occupy space, to awaken the city. However, this, of course, is a call that cannot be heeded by everyone and at the same time. Simply occupying space in the city is not enough to radically undo deeply embedded spatial codes and legacies.

The performance, however, aimed to provoke a public reaction from unexpected spectators. When they asked us what we were doing, I told them that we were reclaiming the right to presence, the right to loiter – with a brief explanation of the theoretical underpinnings. Perhaps they went away with the same sentiments as the private security guard, but maybe they left with a new idea of what it meant to give meaning to a highly deterred act, momentarily offering a new and contingent vision for protecting and celebrating stillness across the city.

1   Onomatopee (2020) "Rights Of Way: The body as witness in public space" [www.onomatopee.net/exhibition/ rights-of-way/]

2   Rendell, J. (2000) *"Bazaar Beauties" or "Pleasure Is Our Pursuit": A Spatial Story of Exchange.* in I. Borden, J. Kerr, J. Rendell (eds.), The Unknown City, pp.104-122.

3   Kelly, L. and Vera-Gray, F. (2020) "Contested gendered space: public sexual harassment and women's safety work". *International Journal of Comparative And Applied Criminal Justice*, 44(4): 265-275. [www.tandfonline.com/doi/full/10.1080/01924036.2020.1732435]

4   The historical context that underpins much of this research owes an intellectual debt to Jane Rendell's Pursuit of Pleasure: Gender, Space and Architecture in Regency London, published in 2002, which depicts the 'rambler', privileged men who, on their travels, encountered 'highly desirable women known as 'cyprians'. The rambler and the cyprian, portrayed by Rendell, were Eighteenth Century precursors to the better known 'flâneurs' and 'prostitutes' (p.38). On a side note, the etymology of flâneur, defined by the Oxford English Dictionary (2012) derives from the old Norse verb flana, 'to wander with no purpose', the almost exact wording of the definition for loitering, to 'stand or wait around without apparent purpose [or] walk slowly and with no apparent purpose'.

5   Rendell, J. (2002) *The Pursuit of Pleasure: Gender, Space & Architecture in Regency London.* p. 55

6   Solnit, R. (2001) *Wanderlust: A history of Walking.*

7   ibid., p. 427.

8   ibid.

9   Rendell (2002), p. 57.

10 Solnit (2001), p. 235.

11 Oxford Languages (2012) [http://languages.oup.com]

12 Aberg-Riger, A. (2018), "What Is Loitering, Really?", *Bloomberg City Lab* [www.bloomberg.com/news/articles/2018-05-21/what-is-loitering-really]

13 Williams, H. (2011), *Ring Of Steel,* http://henriettawilliams.com/ring-of-steel

PROJECT DIRECTORY

Project Directory foregrounds six propositional projects as alternative approaches and possibilities of performing arts, research and dance to city-making. These are only the first entries in a catalogue of interdisciplinary spatial practices, which means to act as a source of inspiration and consultation for different professionals.

The Beach and the Time

The beach is the place of leisure, work, meetings, sexuality, repression, sleep, play, sun and much more. A territory of instability, transformation and uncertainty. Its thin sand soil forms and deforms to the taste of time and according to desires. The crossing of footprints confuses us, indicates multiple possibilities, hypotheses that occupy the imaginary and defy the possibility of prediction. As the day goes on, so do the wind and the tide so that, at dawn, the territory becomes available again, always open to what will come. The beach makes you think about time, about a way of being and not being.

The Beach and the Time – A Praia E O Tempo – was organised through a combination of two operations: demarcating and repositioning. The first operation consisted of the insertion of a large 31x31m and 50cm high quadrilateral structure that demarcates the work area while serving as a support for the reception of the public. The second operation came from the movement of the existing matter in the place – sand and water – that, once repositioned, gave rise to a new topographic landscape. Combined, the two operations generated a scenario that gradually changed during the Tempo Festival.

The installation was presented in 2018, on the exact same day that more than a hundred million Brazilians went to the polls to elect the current president. In contrast to the rise of conservative thinking represented in the figure of the elected candidate, the project offered to the public a platform for demonstrations of various natures: a 1,000m² public arena at Copacabana Beach as a new topographic landscape with free and unrestricted access, in which every day passers-by and artists gathered around. The project recounts the layers of time, critically positioning itself in relation to the specific political context and presenting itself as an important instrument of reflection and criticism.

Year   2018
Location   Copacabana, Rio de Janeiro, Brazil
Author   gru.a (grupo de arquitetos): Pedro Varella, caio calafate, André Cavendish,
              Júlia carreiro, Isadora Tebaldi
Category   Public installation and performance
Link   http://www.grua.arq.br

Punt.Point

Punt.Point is a project that reflects our awareness of the way individual and collective bodies inhabit, move through, organise and choreograph public space. As practitioners/researchers in residence at the Van Abbemuseum, we studied the way in which people (visitors and staff) position themselves while viewing and working amongst art, and how their physical movements collaborate with and are affected by social codes, rules, and invisible laws of public space. Our work plays with such relations of body and space by prompting ways of positioning or re-positioning ourselves that might celebrate and liberate new relations. Participants engaging with the project receive a yellow pouch containing a cushion, maps, re-positioning diagrams, and a notebook. With this wearable 'toolkit' they are invited to play with various modes of being within the museum while exploring new ways to experience its architecture and connection with each other.

Year	2013–2017 (installed as part of the program 'Storylines')
Location	Eindhoven, Netherlands
Author	Artist Sara Wookey in collaboration with urban designer Rennie Tang and Design Assistant: Gabriela Baka
Category	A performance-based relational artwork
Link	vanabbemuseum.nl/en/programme/programme/moving-the-museum/

City Footfall

There was a time when humankind celebrated the vital role of rhythm through ritual, an acknowledgement of its centrality to cosmos. Relying heavily on the audible and inaudible cycles of the world around us, people learned to tune with the rhythm of their own bodies and surroundings to survive. With city life and advanced technology dominating the landscape of today, rhythm remains still the fundamental motor of the implicit and explicit transactions of life.

Quest Ensemble's composition *City Footfall* is inspired by this notion of the inherent rhythm of the city and the bodies of its inhabitants. The musical idea first struck comes from improvising in a stark underground practice room located in the heart of the Barbican, where the only access to the outside world was a window at eye level. Through that window, we could see the legs and feet of city workers scurrying past at different speeds and paces, at times stopping to take notice of surroundings, or have an encounter with one another. Intuitively, responding to the place and space we were in, the ongoing motion of the city seeped into our musical ideas. The seeds of *City Footfall* began to take shape, as did its story. The trio of Quest Ensemble composes collaboratively, exploring different starting points and methods, and works primarily

without notation, seeing improvisation and composition as part of the same fluid continuum. The beauty of the way the work is constructed lies in dynamism, as each composer can move a musical or conceptual idea forward in unpredictable ways, creating a constant movement. Requiring a special kind of awareness and listening, *City Footfall* is a good example of this dynamism; with a structure that is defined and yet simultaneously lends itself to the moment, the piece evolves and has a new meaning every time we perform within a new space for a new audience.

Music-making and urban life have more parallels than most people realise, both demanding tempo and precision to balance chaos and order, whilst also retaining an essence of improvisation and play. Even when working with a structure in mind, we still have great freedom to respond to the moment and to each other. Resembling the city, *City Footfall* brings out repetitive patterns in dialogue with non-linear events and a more varied background of sound effects. The piece opens on a relentless bass line and groove that highlights the continuous motion of the city and drives the rest of the piece forward. This rhythmic pace encapsulates the joy, excitement and exhaustion of living in a city.

Year   2014
Location   London
Author   Quest Ensemble: Preetha Narayanan, violin; Filipe Sousa, piano; Tara Franks, cello.
Category   musical composition
Link   https://qensemble.bandcamp.com/

Sensuous Society

How the sensuous might support a transition towards a more sustainable future?

By engaging theories on aesthetics and ecology in my artistic practice, Sensuous Society envisions a potential future world governed by aesthetic premises, written as a response to the financial crisis in 2008 and to the on-going ecological emergency. My artistic practice seeks ways to 'democratise the aesthetic', meaning to open access to the sensuous and poetic mode of being in the world. The projects of Dome of Visions and Sisters Academy – by Sisters Hope – both share this intention, and they each, in different ways, tease out ways to accomplish that. Very roughly put, the dome-shaped temporary construction Dome of Visions provides a sensuous and poetic space to the general public for aesthetic contribution and creation due to its open curatorial framework, and Sisters Academy works through a performance method evoking the sensuous and poetic aspects of our being within a highly immersive performance-installationary space. Both projects have been research-based from the beginning, generating expansive, reflective, in-situ material from the participants. This material, extracted as empirical data, was further analysed theoretically through a three-phased ritual process and three analytical frameworks of ecologies.

In this project, art is understood as a cultivation of the aesthetic and thus as a space for intensified sensuous experience, perception and cognition. The sensuous experience and realization of the world, furthermore, allows for the poetic mode of being to emerge, characterized by openness, more specifically to something else and more than to the merely physically and empirically measurable. In the analyses of the subtracted in-situ data, which was generated while the participants were in a sensuous and poetic mode, I asked the research question: What is the impact of Dome of Visions' and Sisters Academy's evocation of the aesthetic on the participants? And what does that tell us about how the aesthetic, and thus the sensuous, might support the transition towards a more sustainable future?

Year	2012–2020
Location	Copenhagen
Author	Gry Worre Hallberg
Category	Research in experimental performance
Link	https://sensuoussociety.org

Street Pantone

How can we live individually but together in the shared spaces of cities where most of us live? Redrawing fringe areas, playing with flows, exploring the architectural and sensitive nature of the urban context, questioning void and waste. Weaving with a variety of speeds and scales, a dancer with his monochrome veil, elongated as the tab of a colour chart, reveals the plasticity of spaces, unfurling the Pantone like an ephemeral phantom that fits in a suitcase. The dancer challenges the activity of the street, invents constructive, eloquent gestures and images modified by movement, inviting inhabitants and bodies to meet.

At once monumental but compact, elastic, colourful, elegant and adventurous, fragile but persistent. Street Pantone artefact, made of 30m long and 3m wide lycra, is a fabric used in dance, such as sports costumes. Through minimal resource approach, the fabric carries symbols, necessities of human conditions such as clothing, shelter, curtain or carpet, aesthetic references such as classic drapes, folds and flags, and architectural desires. As a nomadic and dynamic vector, both a link and a border, it challenges the artifice, metamorphoses reality and landscape, and becomes a paintbrush, a spectrum, an actor, or the leitmotiv of a comic strip, turning itself permeable to situations, travelling, inventing scores, rhythms and states of the day.

Street Pantone is an individual duet in common spaces, creating ephemeral monumental installations in an itinerant form, linking to the context, history and identity of heritage places, cities or landscapes, and interacting with the audience and the inhabitants of these places. It can evoke a sailor and his sail, a painter and his colour, a traveller and his load, a worker on a building site, an architect with his measurements, volumes, points and lines, and the basic duality of dance between impulse and gravitation.

Year   2015 – 2020
Location   Prague, Geneva, Marseille, Périgueux
Author   Gilles Viandier
Category   performance, dance, installation
Link   https://www.numberproject.net

Dancing Architects

Approaching architecture *through* choreography and *as* choreography, we cross-pollinate contemporary dance with architecture. Operating as a transdisciplinary research platform, our curiosity is to experiment with movement as both an agency and a medium for exploring the creative process itself – an open possibility towards new ways of perceiving, experiencing, articulating, conceiving, communicating and creating architecture.

Direct engagement with movement is an alternative form of learning by doing. It awakens our physical spatial intelligence, enabling us to extend our sensibility and awareness towards more relational perspectives. By moving and being moved with intentions, we learn to express and communicate our embodied ideas with urgency and poetry that manifest in various manners. Becoming the medium brings changes as to how we see, interpret and relate to the shifting world around us.

Working with dance and choreography also enables us to naturally engage with human senses and emotions; the intangibles and invisibles which are invaluable aspects of the experience of space and of life. When we move together, we also build trust to each other via togetherness and beyond any individual differences. Amidst various transformative learning experiences,

we, in Dancing Architects, also hope to inspire dialogues on empathy and care in architecture contributing to our future wellbeing and happiness.

Learning from and collaborating with many dancers and choreographers over the long searching period, various ideas were tested in movement workshops, dialogues, performances and events. After a long period of incubation, our research platform was finally shaped in 2019 when Julie Anne Stanzak, a long-term dancer at the legendary German dance theatre company Tanztheater Wuppertal Pina Bausch, joined forces to explore this transdisciplinary vision together.

Dancing Architects' first summer workshop Architectural Body // Urban Choreography took place in Apulia in Italy in July 2019. The streetscape of the White City of Ostuni was the stage for our urban choreography. With the choreographic inhabitation as a method to read the city, we explored the urban construct and history, textures, materiality, sound, and activities taking place, before bringing them back to the studio where the participants interpreted and re-enacted the embodied ideas in the new context, weaving a travelling narrative of performance as experimental architectural dialogue. We will keep exploring different cities in the world by moving; and moving together.

Year	2019–ongoing
Location	Based in London, workshop in various cities
Author	Takako Hasegawa
Category	Transdisciplinary platform
Link	https://www.dancingarchitects.org

Contributors

Adesola Akinleye
is an interdisciplinary artist-scholar and choreographer, and a Senior Lecture at Middlesex University, running a web-based/online BA and MA course for professional working artists. She is a Research Fellow with Theatrum Mundi and visiting lecturer at Central Saint Martins (UAL), Spatial Practices Department. She is Visiting Artist 2020–2022 at Center for Art, Science & Technology (CAST) MIT and Research Affiliate at Art, Culture and Technology (ACT), MIT. Akinleye has published in the field of dance scholarship as well as cultural and social studies.

Andrea Cetrulo
is associate Programme Curator at Theatrum Mundi, and has an affinity for architecture, philosophy, the Atlantic Ocean, and wine. She studied Sociology at the University of Barcelona, and Urban Studies at University College London. She shares her life-long fascination with the occult through her monthly show on Noods, a UK independent radio station.

Blanca Pujals
is an architect, spatial researcher and critical writer. Her cross-disciplinary practice uses spatial research and critical analysis to engage with questions around the geographies of power on bodies and territories, policies of scientific and technological knowledge production, as well as transnational politics, developing tools for undertaking analysis through different visual and sonic devices. Her work encompasses film, architecture, lecturing, curatorial projects, teaching and critical writing.

Cecily Chua
is an Associate at Theatrum Mundi, where she specialises in research and editorial. She has a background in architecture and her works focuses on the cultural life of our towns and cities, seeking to understand people's lived experiences of their urban environments and the subcultures that evolve from them. Her work has been exhibited internationally at the Architecture and Urbanism Biennales of Seoul, Buenos Aires, and Glasgow.

Elahe Karimnia
is an Associate at Theatrum Mundi leading on Urban Research and Spatial Practice. She is a practiced architect and urban designer, writer and researcher, with a PhD in Urban Studies from KTH School of Architecture, where she is a guest teacher in critical urban theory. She is interested in designing publicness with plural narratives and multiple temporalities, experimental methods and interdisciplinary approaches. Elahe has studied and worked in Tehran, Stockholm, Toronto and London.

Ellie Cosgrave
is a Lecturer in Urban Innovation and Policy at UCL's department for Science Technology Engineering and Public Policy (STEaPP), where she is co-director of the Urban Innovation and Policy Lab. She is also an outspoken advocate and campaigner for increasing the quality of women's health services. She is a BBC broadcaster, presenting the *Tomorrow's World* Podcast and the BBC World Service series My Perfect City.

Fani Kostourou
is an Associate at Theatrum Mundi leading on Research, Design and Creative Development. She is an architect and urbanist, holding a PhD from UCL Bartlett and teaches at Cardiff University, the University for the Creative Arts, and UAL Central Saint Martins. Fani conducts research, engages in curatorial and editorial work, and publishes internationally on design, computation, critical and interdisciplinary spatial theories, housing, and urban cultures.

Giuditta Vendrame
through her work explores the intersections between design, art practice and legal systems, focusing on personhood, space and mobility. She is based in the Netherlands and tutors at Design Academy Eindhoven. Her work has been exhibited and presented in international contexts including: Walker Art Center, Philadelphia Museum of Art, Van Abbemuseum Eindhoven, Venice Architecture Biennale, RMIT Gallery Melbourne, OCAT Shenzhen.

John Bingham-Hall
is Director of Theatrum Mundi and an independent researcher interested in performances, infrastructures, and technologies of shared life in the city. With a background in music (Goldsmiths) and architectural theory (UCL Bartlett), he works across artistic, spatial and critical humanities to question and participate in the making of the urban public sphere. Alongside initiating projects with Theatrum Mundi, he has collaborated on research projects at LSE and Oxford, taught at CSM and UCL, published writing across scholarly and arts platforms; and organised queer cultural events.

Lisa Sandlos
is on faculty at York University in Toronto, Canada where she holds a PhD in Gender, Feminist and Women's Studies and an MA in Dance. She is also a Certified Movement Analyst (CMA) through the Laban Institute of Movement Studies (LIMS). Over her thirty-year career as a dance artist and educator, she has been a keen interdisciplinary collaborator in dozens of community and professional arts projects.

Luke Gregory-Jones
graduated with an MA in Art and Politics from Goldsmiths, University of London in 2017, developing a practice that explores collaborative approaches to moving in and through space. Luke delivers collaborative walking projects around East London and also works at Whitechapel Gallery.

Marcos Villalba
is a graphic designer and photographer born in Madrid.
He graduated from Central Saint Martins (UAL) in 2008
and spent the following decade working in London. He
currently resides in Montevideo, Uruguay, where he runs
a design studio working with clients accross the fields
of art, culture and education, as well as self-initiated
projects focused on architecture and urbanism. He
has been collaborating with Theatrum Mundi in digital
projects, publications and exhibition design.

Matthias Sperling
is a Canadian/German artist, choreographer and
performer living and working in London, UK. His work
includes creating performances in theatre, gallery and
museum contexts, as well as extending to curatorial
work and scientific research collaborations. His work
has been presented at Sadler's Wells, Tate Modern,
Southbank Centre, Royal Opera House, Wellcome Collection, Dance Umbrella and Nottdance, among others.

Paolo Patelli
manipulates spatial and artistic practice. His work is
research-driven, empirically scaffolded in ethnographic
observations, media excavations and archival mediations.
He was a 2020/2021 Fellow at the Akademie Schloss
Solitude, a 2019/2020 Research Fellow at Het Nieuwe
Instituut, and artist-in-residence at the Jan van Eyck
Academie in Maastricht (2017/18). He holds a PhD from
Politecnico di Milano (2015) and teaches at Sandberg
Instituut and at Design Academy Eindhoven. He exhibits
and publishes internationally.

Paul Setúbal
explores the body as an important structure for discussions that permeate situations of conflict. His research
is based on different types of media such as sculpture,
installation, drawing, painting, video, photography and
performance, addressing the problems and symbologies
of the body in contemporary society: its use, control,
violence, resistance, abuse and power relationships.
His work has been included in group exhibitions at:
Museu de Arte Moderna, São Paulo; Museu de Arte do
Rio; Museum of Old and New Art, Tasmania; HOME,
Manchester; Sesc Pompéia, São Paulo.

Pepa Ubera
is an artist and dancer based in London. In her interdisciplinary practice she works with choreography,
video, site specific, text and light. Pepa's current
research explores narratives of progress in relation to
the sensual body, the non-human and technology. She
works internationally including Chile, Australia and
across Europe. In the UK she has presented work at Tate
Modern and Sadler's Wells Theatre. Ubera is a Sadlers
Well's Summer University artist (2015-2018) and runs
Kimera studio.

Rebecca Faulkner
is a spatial practitioner, currently studying for her
M Arch: Architecture at Central Saint Martins (UAL),
London. A self-proclaimed researcher and writer,
Rebecca's practice intersects an emerging field of
performative-thinking and urbanism (built on the rich
foundation of critical feminist research and activism).
Through writing and performance-based work, Rebecca
explores the gendering and governing of public space,
unpicking themes of permission, privilege, surveillance,
and the technological gaze and how these conditions
contribute to our understanding of self and the city.

Rennie Tang
is a designer and educator based in Los Angeles. Her
practice-based research interests include the investigation of choreographic and sonic tools as methods
for architectural/landscape/urban design, health and
well-being in landscapes and intergenerational play;
this research is fueled by collaborations with choreographers, sound and visual artists, movement analysts and
occupational therapists.

Richard Sennett
is a sociologist, musician and Theatrum Mundi founder,
and currently serves as Senior Advisor to the United
Nations on its Program on Climate Change and Cities.
He is Senior Fellow at the Center on Capitalism and
Society at Columbia University and Visiting Professor of
Urban Studies at MIT. Previously, he founded the New
York Institute for the Humanities, taught at New York
University and at the London School of Economics, and
served as President of the American Council on Work.
Over the course of the last five decades, he has written
several books about social life in cities, changes in
labour, and social theory.

Editorial: Elahe Karimnia, Fani Kostourou
Concept: Rebecca Faulkner, Elahe Karimnia,
　　　　　Fani Kostourou, John Bingham-Hall
Design: Marcos Villalba
Typesetting: Santiago Confalonieri
Illustrations: Cecily Chua
Proofreading: The Book Edit
Typeface: Neue Haas Unica
Printing: Colour Options

Image captions and credits
Front cover: illustration © Cecily Chua
p. 5,7,25,27,39,41,49,51 illustrations © Cecily Chua
pp. 16-18 How Does the City Move You © Stephen Wright
p. 24 Taking Them Down © Elahe Karimnia
p. 33 Laban Score For Un-walling The City
© Rebbie Tang and Lisa Sandlos
p. 34 Proposal For A New Public Sculpture
© Paolo Patelli and Giuditta Vendrame
pp. 37-38 Friction Atlas. Traces removed from Novi Trg.
Moderna Galerija, Ljubljana, 2014 © Paolo Patelli and
Giuditta Vendrame
p. 58 Improvisatory Design © Luke Gregory-Jones
p. 62 The Act of Loitering portrait: Jackie (top left), Kanel
(top right), Silvia (bottom) © Rebecca Faulkner
p. 64 The Act of Loitering portrait © Rebecca Faulkner
p. 66 The Beach and the Time © Rafael SAlim
p. 67 The Beach and the Time © Elisa Mendes
p. 68 Window © Niek Tijsseklanesn
p. 69 Pouch and content © Gabriella Baka
pp. 70-71 collage © Marcos Villalba
pp. 72-73 Sisters Hope © I diana lindhardt
pp. 74-75 Street Pantone © Gilles Viandier
pp. 76-77 Dancing Architects © Dancing Architects

We would like to thank all the contributors for the pro-
vision of images and for the permission of (re)printing
selected texts and projects, and the partner organisations and individuals who have collaborated with Theatrum Mundi in the work presented in this edition:

Adam Kaasa, Adesola Akinleye, Akil Scafe-Smith,
Andrea Cetrulo, Blanca Pujals, Carlos Maria Romero,
Candoco Dance Company, CSM Spatial Practices,
Dominick Bagnato, Elahe Karimnia, Ellie Cosgrave, Fani
Kostourou, Future Architecture, Gilles Viandier, Gascia
Ouzounian, Giuditta Vendrame, Gry Worre Hallberg,
James Anderson, Joel Brown, John Bingham-Hall, Jorge
Saavedra Utman, Joselyne Contreras, Hagit Yakira,
Julie Desprairies, Kiera Blakey, Lauren Wright, Lisa
Sandlos, Luke Gregory-Jones, Matthias Sperling, Paolo
Patelli, Paul Setúbal, Pedro Varella, Pepa Ubera, Preetha
Narayanan, Rebecca Faulkner, Rennie Tang, Richard
Sennett, Rosemary Lee, Sara Adhitya, Sara Wookey, Sam
Causer, Siobhan Davies, Siobhan Davies Dance, Takako
Hasagawa, The Oxford Research Centre for the Humani-
ties, UCL City Leadership Laboratory.

Friends of Theatrum Mundi
(see https://theatrum-mundi.org/membership/)
CSM MA Cities

The publication Embodying Otherness is part of the
Future Architecture platform programme co-funded by
the Creative Europe Programme of the European Union.
The content of this publication reflects the views of the
authors and can in no way be taken to reflect the views
of the European Union.

Theatrum Mundi
c/o Groupwork
15a Clerkenwell Close
EC1R 0AA
London, UK

Theatrum Mundi Europe
59 Rue du Département
75018
Paris, France

www.theatrum-mundi.org

ISBN 978-1-9161864-4-6

This publication is part of Theatrum Mundi Editions,
a quarterly series reflecting current streams and
new directions in our research, led by our team and
collaborators, and shared with our members. Editions
are generously supported by the Friends of Theatrum
Mundi, who are listed in the acknowledgments.

Co-funded by the
Creative Europe Programme
of the European Union